# Adam of Ifé
*Black Women in Praise of Black Men*

# *Adam of Ifé*

## Black Women in Praise of Black Men

### Poems

*Edited and with a Foreword by*
## Naomi Long Madgett

*Illustrated by*
Carl Owens

*Cover Art by*
Paul Goodnight

LOTUS PRESS
Detroit

p. 13A

First Edition
Second Printing, November, 1992


International Standard Book Number 0-916418-80-4
Library of Congress Catalog Card Number 91-61410


Printed in the United States of America

LOTUS PRESS, INC.
Post Office Box 21607
Detroit, Michigan 48221

*To all the brothers*
*with love*

# Foreword

When I mentioned to a female acquaintance my plan to compile this anthology, she greeted the news with a grunt, then asked, "Do you think you'll get any material?" The response of another friend was a short, brittle laugh, followed by: "You must be expecting a teeny- *tiny* little book." These reactions came as no surprise; they were the all too frequent indications that many African-American women have found their relationships with their men disastrous. Personal statements about the reputed worthlessness of black men proliferate, while daily media reports remind us of the extent to which they have fallen.

Nevertheless, I believe that, for every negative example of black manhood caught in the public spotlight, there are numerous others who are quietly living exemplary lives without ever seeing their names in print. Feeling a need to bring *them* out of the shadows and tell them, "We see you; we know you are there, and we appreciate your presence in our lives," I decided to pay tribute to them through poetry, the means that is most natural for me, and so, *Adam of Ifé* was conceived.

I set out to reach as many black women poets as possible, either through direct contact or through press releases to magazines and journals, for it was important to me to solicit fresh material. Far too many anthologists have drawn their material entirely from other anthologies. As a result, poets whose names readers recognize are often known only for the same three or four poems that have been reprinted to death for years, or even decades, while their more recent work remains relatively unknown. In the meantime, many deserving newer poets go unnoticed.

Some of the periodicals contacted published notices; some, arguing that this information should be paid advertising, did not. At least one editor with good intentions simply procrastinated and let the press release languish on his desk. But that old reliable grapevine got busy, one poet passing on the word to others. The response was tremendous. Some poets went to the trouble to include encouraging notes about the need for such a project. I regret that we were not able to reach all those who might have wished to contribute and to use every entry that did come in, but I am grateful to all who responded, even though they may not be among the fifty-five poets whose work is represented here.

While concentrating on positive images of black manhood, we have not forgotten our other brothers who have fallen by the wayside. They did not arrive at their present state without help. When I was teaching Afro-American literature, I discovered as one of the recurring themes the emasculation of the black male. "Truant" by Claude McKay and "Health Card" by Frank Yerby are just two fictional illustrations. The American system has conspired, since the first African set foot on this soil, to deprive him of his humanity. What other immigrant in world history has ever been defined *legally* as only "three-fifths of a man"? White fiction writers have traditionally stereotyped him in so many undignified and sometimes vicious roles that it would be difficult to recognize him as a man like any other. (See Sterling Brown's essay, "A Century of Negro Portraiture in American Literature"[1] for some of these images.)

During slavery, the black male had little opportunity to shoulder responsibility. Since it was traditionally believed that only women could nurture children, the presence of a man in a household was deemed unnecessary and perhaps even dangerous. As much as a black father might have wished to care for and train his children, he often was permitted little or no contact with them. Even where families were kept intact, the father was powerless to protect his wife and female children from sexual exploitation by master or overseer. What degradation and shame he must have felt to find himself in a position of such impotence! The segregationists who railed against race-mixing certainly did not object to the union of a white male with an African female; the variety of skin tones, hair textures, and other features apparent among African-Americans today attests to the popularity of the Southern man's most noble sport! It was, of course, the reversal of this arrangement — the involvement of a black man with a white woman — that always has been the most widely protected taboo in this country, for sex is indeed power, and the black man must never be granted the privilege of competing with a white man on this level. Furthermore, the myth of racial inferiority could not stand to be put to a test for if it were, it would be necessary to answer the

---

[1]In *The Massachusetts Review* (Winter, 1966), reprinted in *Black Voices,* edited by Abraham Chapman (The New American Library, 1968).

question of why a white woman would *want* to sleep with a black man if he was truly inferior. The black man had to be portrayed as subhuman and deprived of his freedom of choice and movement in order to prevent his becoming a threat to the white male ego.

From Emancipation to the Civil Rights Movement — and even into the present — the power structure has used any means necessary to keep the black male from occupying his rightful place in society, fearing that, given an equal opportunity, the black man might surpass his white brother. By the beginning of the century, a pattern of inequality of opportunity had been firmly established. If education was the key to advancement, then it must be rendered useless to the black male. Therefore, if a struggling family, by pooling all its resources, could manage to send only one child to college, a daughter was likely to be chosen, even though a son might have been the eldest child, for experience had proved that, while a young woman could sometimes find employment commensurate with her training and ability, her brother would not be so fortunate. How many black men only a generation ago, possessing impressive natural ability and/or holding a college degree, were forced into specific types of manual labor or service jobs which were considered beneath the dignity of their white neighbors. Except for self-employed professionals, the most prestigious kind of male employment for blacks in northern cities was postal work. Even the professionals were limited; the black doctor, not being permitted to serve on the staff of his local hospital, was forced to either send his patients to white doctors for specialized care and surgery or join forces with some of his colleagues to establish their own inadequate hospitals.

The African-American woman, on the other hand, posing no threat in the workplace, could often use her education to advance as teacher, nurse, social worker, or secretary, professions traditionally engaged in by females. The result of this inequality of opportunity between the sexes led to a family structure in which the wife was often better employed and better paid than her spouse. That such a disadvantage could lead a man to try to boost his own self- esteem by attempting to "knock down to size" the female who had surpassed him does not come as a surprise, considering that, in spite of the Women's Movement, we still live in a male-dominated society.

In the last few years we have witnessed a dramatic change in the employment opportunities available to young black men. Yet as a group, they are worse off than ever before. Reading the statistics on school failure, drug addiction, family irresponsibility, and crime, we might easily conclude that the fault is not in these men's now plentiful stars but in themselves. While agreeing that, in some cases, no better explanation is available, we must also concede that history and its effects cannot be erased, nor are its scars quick to heal. Many young males are trapped in a syndrome of failure and despair so familiar to them that only a will stronger than they possess could liberate them.

Considering the disproportionate number of young black women who are currently rearing families alone, one might be tempted to blame them for their sons' failures. No one would deny that home training and parental discipline are extremely important to a child's development, but I am wary of generalizations. From my experience and observation, I find that homes with both parents present are no guarantee that a child will turn out well, even when those parents provide an ideal moral environment. The "broken home" has too long taken the blame for problems whose roots may lie elsewhere. I am convinced that, in spite of those very visible parents who are neglectful, if not downright abusive, the majority of single mothers are doing an admirable job of bringing up their young. Many rise early to drop them off at child care centers, hold down responsible positions, come home to cook and clean, and still manage to find quality time to spend with their offspring. Many more of them than we are willing to recognize are doing their best to teach the same moral values they learned from their own parents.

But this is not the same world of generations past, and today's youth face outside pressures and perils far more critical than those of bygone days. *All* American youth today are at risk, but it is the least prepared of them and the most vulnerable who are most likely to succumb. The absence of positive male role models in the lives of many young men must be addressed with community response.

When we take into account the omissions and distortions inherent in traditional education, it is hardly surprising that many little black boys can perceive nothing in their universe that can thwart their sense of hopelessness and futility. Until very recently, very little that they learned in school related positively to their own identity or encouraged a feeling of self-worth. As far as they could determine from their textbooks, their kind simply did not exist. School systems and textbook publishers have now begun to correct past sins, but the changes have not come soon enough to make a difference to those who have already adopted an attitude of no expectation. Until the educational system catches up and teaches the whole truth about black people's contributions to history, literature, art, and science, *all* American children will continue to be educationally and culturally deprived.

Ifé (pronounced EE-fay) is a city in Nigeria where, according to African legend, the deity Odudua (OH-doo-DWAH) created the first man. Since that moment of creation, many men of African descent have forgotten their heritage. During the Sixties, the late Harold G. Lawrence (Kofi Wangara) wrote a poem entitled, "The Mirror,"[1] in which he pictures such a young man looking at his reflection with shame and self-hatred. The speaker in the poem raises the question, "Why do you look at you like that?" knowing the answer very well. Referring to this African creation story, he reminds the youth of his proud and unique history, saying, "When Odudua went to Ifé, / he went to make you—you." I hope that this book will serve as such a reminder to others who may view themselves and their kind negatively.

I have only admiration for those generations of black women who gave support and encouragement to their men, forgave many trespasses against them and kept on going, disciplined their children and held them together as families, and gave unstintingly of their strength and love. One of them, in particular, comes to mind. You will recall the son in Lorraine Hansberry's fine play, *A Raisin in the Sun.* Walter Lee Younger, frustrated by his lack of opportunity, has lost his family's inheritance through a scatterbrain get-rich-quick scheme that failed. You remember his college student sister's disgust as she reviles him for being less than a man. To her insults, Mama replies:

"Child, when do you think is the time to love somebody the most; when they done good and made things easy for everybody? Well then, you ain't through learning — because that ain't the time at all. It's when he's at his lowest and can't believe in hisself 'cause the world done whipped him so. When you starts measuring somebody, measure him right, child, measure him right. Make sure you done taken into account what hills and valleys he come through before he got to wherever he is.[2]

---

[1] In *The Negro History Bulletin* (October, 1962), p. 52.

[2] Copyright © 1958, 1959, 1965, 1966 by Robert Nemiroff. By permission of the estate of Robert Nemiroff.

The women poets in this anthology have expressed their love, support, and compassion for their brothers in a way that I think Lena Younger would have approved. I am grateful to all of them for making this anthology an appropriate celebration of the twentieth anniversary of Lotus Press.

Special thanks go to Titilaya Akanke for her assistance with the typesetting and organization of this material.

I also wish to express my appreciation to those two beautiful brothers, Carl Owens and Paul Goodnight, artists who enthusiastically offered the use of their art for the illustrations and cover of this book.

My husband, Leonard P. Andrews, deserves special thanks for his constant support and for his patience during the various stages of this project's development. For all the encouragement I have received from various sources, I am deeply grateful.

*NLM*
October 3, 1991
September 29, 1992

# Contents

## III. LOVERS

## IV. STREET SCENE

## To Be a Man

*To be a man*
*is to be as strong*
*as a wave breaking*
*over a bed of lava*
*cooling Pelée's wrathful flames*

*and as gentle*
*as the ripples in a tide*
*that cause the mouths*
*of sea anemone*
*to sway without closing.*

*— KARLA FRANCESCA BRUNDAGE*

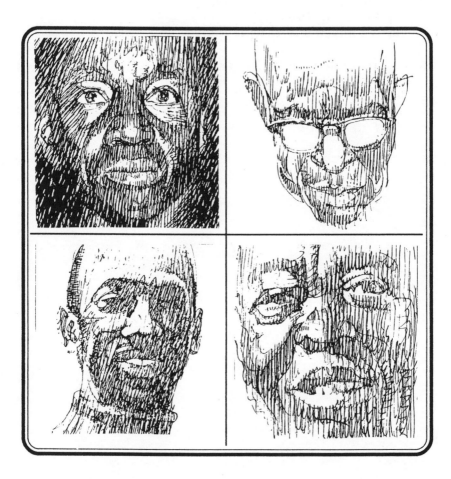

# I

# *Fathers*

"I will name you love
and truth
and beauty"
*(Maketa Groves)*

# Praises

They sing of my father
he is fierce.
His spear is swift.
It pierces the gazelle's heart
killing with elephant strength.

My mother smiles for my father.
She moves, a willow in spring rain.
My father's son rocks in the steps
of her dance. She smiles often.

I dance for my father.
His touch is a feather under the chin.
I bounce in his arms
smelling kola nut and palmwine on his robe.
I dance often.

—IRMA McCLAURIN

# Katumwbe

Maketa, name from my father
Father, what is your name?
Your lips are ripe like purple berries.
Your legs and arms are long and straight
like trees rising from the ground.
Your oblong head glistens, black

Father, what is your name?

You smile, father,
your eyes narrowing
your brow wrinkled
your head slightly inclined.

Father, we have lost the essence
You are named Levi, a jewish name
though your skin is ebony and velvet
as the night

Father, you are named Smith, an english name
though you speak with the tongues of african wisdom

Father, what is your name?

I will name you love
and truth
and beauty
I will name you all that endures, like stone, and wood
and animals of the night
and flowing rivers
and herbs of every kind
I will name you in all the tongues the spirits have given
us to sing
I will name you, as you named me Maketa, and said,
"You do what you want with the last  name!"

I have named us, father

—MAKETA GROVES

# sunflowers and saturdays

daddy sits
in his brown
leather chair,
back straight,
brow tight
behind the
rims of
his glasses.
he studies
my puzzles
with precise
algebraic
words,
printed perfectly
balanced
with the
center of the page.

his hair
waves into
even black
curves,
streaked with
silver
as smooth as
my child-
hood
cuddled in
his lap
on a saturday
afternoon
sneaking a sip
of beer
studying the
red scar
above his
right eye
fixed on
the cross-
word puzzle

*(Continued)*

or speck
of dust
diving into
the tv
screen.

the summers
were longer then,
when i kept
frogs
and turtles
in the shade
of the sunflowers
and the
quaking aspen
daddy planted
my third
spring.

still an
ignorant child
sulking justice,
i build
poems
from chipped
and narrow
fractions.
daddy reads
with the
ambiance
of sunflowers
and saturdays,
yesterday
afternoon

—MELBA JOYCE BOYD

# A Little Black Poem 4 Larry
### *(Especially for Larry Martin)*

A big black man with a big black smile holds
       my smaller black hand and protects me
And his big black mind knows my big black
       dream and his big black love heals
       and soothes me
In God's big black world full of big black sky
       comes a big black gift to redeem me:
A big black man with a big black heart
       holds my smaller black hand and
       protects me.

—LESLIE REESE

# A Father's Teaching

He took small brown hands
and wrapped leather reins
around them

      guided tiny sneakered feet
gently into saddle stirrups
they could barely reach

      walked patiently nearby
guiding a young equestrienne
to the perimeter of life

           That child grew
and took those
reins of control
and
stirrups of direction

crossing many valleys of deception
armored with a father's teaching
being careful to keep balance

and with strength and pride
rode into maturity
secure in her identity.


— ELANA HAYES

# Resurrections (#36)

When I was very small, I had a
rocking chair similar to Father's.
Placed beside his (between him and the
radio that topped the music cabinet),
I would sit and rock beside him as
he read aloud the leading stories
in the evening paper to Mother who
sat across the room in one of the large
velvet and gilt chairs that were a special
joy.

     In the lowering dark, by lamplight,
he forced our attention to the world.
Mother seldom spoke, quietly listening,
now and then answering some question
put to her. When there seemed little of
great interest, he would turn out the
light and quietly chat. Always, these times
surprised me. Matching his voice to the
softness of the night, his was a muted
conversation, and every now and then
hers was an easy laugh that lifted
across the room.

     Such times I liked best;
when we three sat housed in the simple
dark and they took no notice of me.

—GLORIA ODEN

# Even Though We Never Went Camping

When typhoons rage
and spoil my days of paradise
you come with the sun
in your backpack

When the world tries to
take my dreams away
you come with strength,
the potion of all realities

When people try to discredit me
for who I am
you tell me they don't know
a damn thing about me

I never looked at you
as just my father of guidance
but as the man who gave me all
the essentials of life:

camp fire stories (to remind me
most fears lie in mass hysteria)

a flashlight (just in case
I got lost and couldn't see where I was)

a compass (to give me a sense
of direction)

and memories of a family (so
I'll always know what love is)

—MARIA MADISON

# My Dad Is a Magician

**I.**
Frederick Douglass, Crispus Attucks, Toussaint L'Ouverture,
Benjamin Banneker, Martin Luther King, Jr.,
  Dr. Seuss and Curious George,
    Adam, Moses, and Jesus Christ
      but first
      and foremost
      there was
      Daddy.

observe him: making furniture/making a patio/growing
          a garden painting our sky with majesty

on bid whist nights see
  his fancy card shuffles!
    ssccrrdrupp!
    wwhhtipth!
    skckkapptatapptck!
isn't my Dad a genius?
          (and Mommy is jealous of the softness of his hands:
          "Why do men have soft hands and long eyelashes? They
          don't *need* them.")

          "My Dad is a magician!"—I finally announced to my
friends after several unmagical attempts to learn card-shuffling
myself, circa 1967.

**II.**
they say that all little girls adore their fathers/want to marry
          them, in fact
but I never wanted to marry my father and give him a big
          movie star kiss; I never had penis envy.
I liked better/to have some *business* with *my* Dad. business
          like: going places with him/disguised as a little kid/
          when secretly—and maybe Dr. Spock would
          understand but not Dr. Smith who was such a
          ninny—secretly
I was assigned to my father/to march around with him as the

*(Continued)*

Telepathic Witness of his Silence.
I was only pretending to learn how to bait a hook for fishing/I
    knew that, already
I endured the lesson to study my father's cigarette breath:
  what part and particles make that smell?
    notice it doesn't smell that way after a meal.
    notice how the odor is more deadly when you
      mess up and do something wrong for the *11th time*
        but if you'd only done it *10* times you wouldn't
          have to smell his breath when he sighs and tells you to
           go and get the belt/speaking
of belts. my Dad is a very dapper dresser.
    Secretly
I was assigned to my father to march around with him as the
    Telepathic Witness of his Silence.
I knew about everything in the hardware store, already/I was
    only pretending
    to be interested in the nuts and bolts, screwdrivers and
    sandpapers
with luck, my Dad might let me carry the bag home and he
    would know I was his sport.
(remember when I was 8 and Mom decided it was time for me to
learn to ride the bus to my dance class/and I was scared at the bus
stop that day /with busfare in my shoe/heavy with dread . . .)
    and my Dad rescued me without saying a word in the car all
the way downtown and not looking into my face, either, so this
    way we had a cosmic understanding not to tell my mother but
      she found out, anyway/because I got lost on the way
      home. "if you'd let her ride the bus *down* there, Claude,
she would have known how to get back!"

my Dad didn't get to go to Dad School
    because his Dad: Isaac Clinton Reese, Sr. died
    when my Dad was 6.

I just thought I'd come around in 1961 and ask him if he wanted
    me to show him the ropes

and he said yes.
  even though he wanted to become a doctor
he said yes.
  that's why my birth certificate says that my Dad was a 26 year
  old Alabama negro straightener for burroughs, corp.


                                        —LESLIE REESE

*"My Dad Is A Magician"* *is a memoir in progress for Claude Reese.*

# A Real Father
### *(To Papa)*

Some plant a seed and walk away,
never looking back to see
if it will live or die.
They do not hear it cry
or pull the weeds
that seek to choke its breath.

But there was one who said,
"I'll be a man.
I'll clear the soil, nurture this seed
and watch it grow to blossom.
Here I will remain, my child.
We'll face this world together,
whatever the years may bring."

— BURNIECE AVERY

# Papi* Was a Dancing Man
*(Dedicated to Zenithia & Kito)*


Papi was 25 shades blacker than midnight
Blue-black, they called him
        Papi
        was a "pretty-boy"
Skin so smooth . . . . .
He looked like he was carved out of ebony
Papi never just walked
He was smooth like his skin
   moved like a panther
     like the wind
       like a well sung song
Papi was beautiful to watch
   wore his pride like armor
     like a weapon
     like a shield
In cities designed to make him disappear
He wore his blackness like a badge of honor
   moved through the whiter than thou madness
     with the grace of greased lightning
Danced his way across stages
   that tried to bury him
     in the filth of "their" fear
Papi was 25 shades blacker than midnight
The kind of unstoppable Black
   that "they" couldn't hold back
     no matter how much "they" tried
Papi was untouchable
Even when "they" tried to get at him
   by trying to get to me
He danced in "their" faces
   on all "their" sacred places
     and made a joke of "their" ignorance
By stealing "their" shows (on "their "stages), and
   giving unasked for lessons on the real Black Power
     his unshakeable power
       our undeniable survival power

---

*Pronounced "Poppy" in the Spanish-speaking Caribbean.

*(Continued)*    

               Papi
Papi was 25 shades blacker than midnight
25 times blacker than was tolerable
     by terrified white folks
          by immaculate "knee-grow" jet setters
Hair "too bad" to be so confident
     too African looking to be so proud
          too loud to be so arrogant
                too damn Black (or so they said)
But even when Black was
     a never to be spoken word
          "they" couldn't stop his beauty
I mean, like
     when Papi smiled
          even the wind held its breath
And while all the foolish tongues rattled . . . he danced
He danced, and spread his Blackness . . . . .
          across the whiteness of this stolen land
And he danced, and danced, and danced, and danced,
          and kept holding my hand
Held on tight till I was strong enough . . . . .
          to see the light & write this poem
Papi was 25 shades blacker than midnight

                              —AVOTCJA

34

# For My Father:
## On the Gift of Another Eye

Now you have
another eye.
The one you had

wore out after
seventy-six years,
lost its strength,

its focus, its
sense of humor.
It could no longer

find its way
in the light.
It forgot how

to gasp. But
the operation
was a success:

(you took the rosary
though you and God
didn't play the same

horse and His tennis
was never as good
as yours) and you're

home again, alive,
with two fairly good
eyes, ready to resume

a fairly good business
with another fairly good
life in your pocket.

Your sight over the years
has really teased you,
led you to corners

*(Continued)*     35

when you needed
stairwells, wasn't
always to be trusted.

Even your visions
deserted you for a while,
and you forgot how to weep.

And you were brave, honest:
you didn't complain. (I
admire you for that, that

was beautiful.) But this
eye given in the dark
by some secret person

may lead you into a blindness
that might be a gift beyond
a 20/20 dream: for suppose

the donor were a billiard
player, a fireman, a young
mother, or better still,

a magician? The possibilities
are stunning! though now
for a while you will be

in emptiness (no news is good);
angels will dance about
the rising retina, illusions

will enter your body
like water, colors will come
in prayers, peaceably enforced,

sound will slip into your brain
with slippers on. Gloucester will
weep in your closet. (You will give

him a silver dollar for ice-cream.)
Yet nothing will be disturbed.
Not really. The matters of men

under calm recovery from
sleepwalking will all converge
on a single movement of the cornea,

a quiver in the clock,
and you, grand and unfinished,
the half-moon blooming

in your jaw, will in the night
whisper your tired and galloping
visions to a second sight.


— DOLORES KENDRICK

# Search

I look for my father in old men's faces
everywhere;
I don't know what I hope to find
in the hard, wrinkled visages
that resemble my father's
but I keep looking anyway . . .

because it's sometimes hard
and unfair that he left me after only 25 years
when I was unprepared.

I look for my father in old men's faces
because I miss his wisdom
and guidance, and,

though I've made it two years
without him

I keep looking anyway.

—JOHARI MAHASIN RASHAD

## Poem for My Father

He stood but 5'10"
yet cast a giant shadow

Grabbed a hold of life
and wouldn't let go

Defied death twenty times over,
stared it straight in the eye
And said "Get away from me"

Scrappy was invincible.

Entered a room
and flashed a hundred watts
of brilliant light and warmth,
healed hearts, touched lives,
lifted spirits,

What cha say!

Fondly known as
"the colored cyclone"
Thomas Waudell Pierce

cast a giant shadow
cast a giant shadow
cast a giant shadow . . .

—ERICA ANNETTE PIERCE

*Thomas W. Pierce died Sunday, December 17, 1989.*

# Seasons

Old man
bent, gnarled, broken.

Old man
easing into clothes
dusty, old
as if left lying
for a season.

Old man
forgotten, forsaken,
has paid his dues
proudly.

—ROSALIE SHANNON

# j. harrington
## good/man, mississippi's son

i think about him
with a softening of the heart now

it wasn't always that way

there was a rage within him
i couldn't understand
an unbridled fury
which i met
as a child
with a child's consternation

i raged against his rage
was furious with his fury
unable to understand
the profundity of his situation

he had experienced things as a man
i could in no way
                    comprehend

he had heard
jim/crow bout strange fruit
while chains ganged him

he had had to wade
through oceans of cotton
travel down miles of mules
while balancing pounds of crackers
on his back

roadblocks to dignity and
shattered dreams of
40 acres and a mule proved
too tough a row to hoe

frustration brought a demon home
turned family into battleground

*(Continued)*

he opted for total eclipse
cause moonshine
brought on sweet amnesia
while sunshine
jogged the memory

my heart
no longer hardened

my mind
no longer clouded
          and confused
understands now

          he is
          what he is

          all he can ever be
          and no more


                    —A. WANJIKU H. REYNOLDS

# This  Warrior

This warrior sits
in an overstuffed chair
by the checkerboard
after fried chicken and greens
pats his belly
to the sounds of television
and tells Momma
everything was good
Retired after forty years
as Negro janitor
he sits now
remembering curses
held back by smiles
that cracked his soul
How he put on
with his overalls
an armor for the world
Became a diplomat
a four star general
on city battlegrounds
He sits now
satisfied to hear
his quiet bargainings
become in us a battle cry

This warrior
understands being misunderstood
Despite baptisms of hate
and our condescending love
has endured

—PAULETTE CHILDRESS WHITE

43

# The Coach
*In memory of Thomas Verdell*

Magical roles you played
squeezing stones for water
upon the scenes of my life.

How should we know you?
Shall we remember scores
and games of victorious men—
winners all, by your might?

Your tally begins with negative numbers:

> -10, miners on strike and union bombings
>         in Alabama
> -9,  Chicago streets, southside
> -8,  a BLACK man among Negro elites:

>> such measured weights
>> for the ankles of a runner
>> "fleetfoot" at Northwestern,
>> cleaning a mascot cage.

Magical roles you played,
man of my birth,
making me fearless
before white might,
cloaking me in gentle dark.

> No dirge of slack tempo
> shall ferry you off—
> no veils or drapes
> or sounding woe.

Throw down the SANDS of
our tune under laced shoes.
I will DANCE my tributes
"on the sunny side of the street."

—SATIAFA (VIVIAN VERDELL GORDON)

44

# My Father
*(In memory of Kelly Miller)*

With springtime my father comes alive
In the lilac bush he planted
At the kitchen door that we
Might hear the plain voice
Of Walt Whitman burst
Through the bloom.
In the season's green-tipped
Hedge, he lives again.

Today I walked beside a river
Breaking up with early thaw.
I closed my eyes to see
The ship from up the
Spring branch that he promised
Would be released one high March day
And bring down to port the treasures
Mined from mother wit and lore.
I learned the passengers in turn:
Torn sailors escaped
From a Cyclops eye,
A boy who grasped a keen-edged plot
In the apple-scented dark,
And the girl — half child, half woman —
Counting off six tiny seeds
To assure each year another spring.

Now I live in the flow of that green time,
And my father lives there too.

—MAY MILLER

# He Lives in Me

*In memory of Clarence Marcellus Long, Sr.*

My father was a strong and stalwart man.
Slight of build, he towered over cities
and had the might of armies.
Light of skin, he was the blackest man I knew:
In the unbeautiful years, he taught me pride;
when despair was ready to engulf me,
he rescued me with hope. By his hands,
in his arms, I was immersed in waters
of integrity and truth.
I learned my lessons at his knee:
> The just shall live by faith . . . .
> If a beggar asks for food but isn't hungry,
>> that's *his* problem. If you turn him away
>> and he really is, it's *yours* . . .
>> (and it isn't your responsibility
>> to take the measure of his guile
>> or honest need).
> If you see a toy with jagged edges
>> (any obstruction)
>> dropped on the floor or in the way,
>> it doesn't matter if *you* put it there
>> or not; you *see* it; you must remove it or
>> you're just as guilty (maybe more so)
>> as the one who left it there . . . .

I am my father's daughter. I make no apologies
for being who I am, for having learned integrity
early in life — make no excuses that my neighborhood
was haven because my parents loved me
and loved each other
and made our home "rock in a weary land."

I go out of my way
to kick banana peels or broken glass
from sidewalks — try to remove obstacles, no matter
who put them there. I will not apologize . . . .

I cannot speak of him in metaphor or symbol.
My father was upright, noble, and uncompromised,
and he gave me all I needed to be proud,
moral, and black — and whole. I can only praise him now
with hallelujahs, trumpets, cymbals, and drums.

— NAOMI LONG MADGETT

## Papa

*(For Henry Walls,*
*November 3, 1901-November 23, 1979)*

Papa,
when men like you die
the streets howl.
torn from this page
the wind that left
your mark on us.
I search
I look for answers
I hear your wise voice
penetrating this plane
of circumstance
and wonder

when men like you die
what will happen
to the rest of us?
who will dictate order to us?
you, who gave order to chaos
in being simply what you were—
who will dictate order
but the orderly?

when men like you,
men who carried mountains
on their shoulders
men who lifted up the sky
men whose tears turned to rain
when you leave us
asleep in the great whore's
petrified womb
stoned,
faltering in our egos
falling like tin soldiers
in an avalanche

when men like you
slip away in the night

48

without our lessons complete
lost in meaning,
our need of a parable:
that was you, Papa
a sign within our souls
that the will though
made of iron is gentle
as real men
are soft rays of light
real men
who are not afraid to love
real men
who do not know what fear is:
that was you, Papa.
who will mend our socks?

when men like you,
men with steel in their backs
men of muscle and teeth
and old folk wisdom
men who carried mountains
on their shoulders
men who lifted up the sky
men whose tears turned to rain
whose memories turned to rainbows
to let us know
the door of heaven
is open still
like your eyes were
when I saw you last . . . .

Papa,
when men like you
go away from us
leaving punks and faggots
in their stead
I wonder
what will happen
to the rest of us
how far  how long
can we go on
distended roots
where somewhere on the

*(Continued)*     49

lonesome road to freedom things
the heart was lost
who will teach us?
who will guide us home?

when men like you leave us
I know it won't be long
before the gospel train
will come and join you
at our Lord's throne.

—NUBIA KAI

# II

# *Brothers, Sons and Other Youth*

"Hug your brother, little sister,
hug him hard."

*(Johari Mahasin Rashad)*

"I will not let them
take you"

*(Opal Palmer Adisa)*

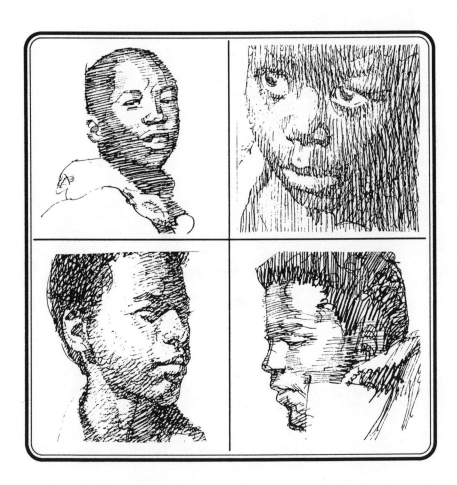

# In Knowledge of Young Boys

i knew you before you had a mother,
when you were newtlike, swimming,
a horrible brain in water.
i knew you when your connections
belonged only to yourself,
when you had no history
to hook on to,
barnacle,
when you had no sustenance of metal
when you had no boat to travel
when you stayed in the same
place, treading the question;
i knew you when you were all
eyes and cocktail,
blank as the sky of a mind,
a root, neither ground nor placental;
not yet
red with the cut nor astonished
by pain, one terrible eye
open in the center of your head
to night, turning, and the stars
blinked like a cat. we swam
in the last trickle of champagne
before we knew breastmilk — we
shared the night of the closet,
the parasitic
closing on our thumbprint,
we were smudged in a yellow book.

son, we were oak without
mouth, uncut, we were
brave before memory.

— TOI DERRICOTTE

# birthday
### for john hays

born
on the winds
of december

you were a
circled forecast

an avalanche of
good news

your warmth gusting
like forced blooms


— HILDA VEST

# Oronde

The tangles on my baby's head
are curious
and beautiful.
His eyes
are circles of sweet mischief.
My hand of gentle Motherlove
smooths a curve of tender cheek
and the smile he gives
is truer than words
he will someday speak.

Golden sun rains down on us
and I will always remember
this moment,
richly painted on the fabric
of my clinging thought,
as even now he struggles
to free himself,
to run away
from me.

— PAULETTE CHILDRESS WHITE

## Precious Flowers

He brings me weeds
blades of grass even
small twigs of trees
He calls them flowers
(Mommy I brought you flowers)
too young yet to appreciate
the beauty of the rose
or the sweet smell of honeysuckle
He hands them to me
stands back and waits for his price
to be paid (always the same)
a gratuitous hug and smile
He brings me weeds
small twigs and clumps of grass
Mommy I brought you flowers
the most precious I have ever seen
and when I open my kitchen window
and see them lying proudly in a bowl
my heart rejoices

— GRETA DELPHINE WHITE

# My Gift to You

My gift to you — a ring

open-sided

like arms to encircle you
with space to allow you to grow
to enclose you, but not so completely
that you have no room to expand.

My gift to you — a ring

open-sided

to remind you of my love
always ready to bring you inside
like arms to encircle you
with space to allow you to grow.

—JOHARI MAHASIN RASHAD

# Waiting

He left the back gate open
so Benj could come back home
Every night from my upstairs window
I watched it swing in the breeze
as the boy with the lost dog
grieved in his room

Silent now in the shade of years
the gate is closed
pining for the touch
of the grown boy
returning home

—MARILYN ELAIN CARMEN (AISHA ESHE)

# I Will Not Let Them Take You
*(for jawara)*


tell them
tell them loud and clear
i will not let them
take you

tell them
tell them your mother is
a crazy jamaican woman
who will wage war
for her children
so tell them
tell them now
i will not surrender
you to the streets
i will not give you over
to dope dealers.
i will not relinquish
you to the cops
who target you because
you are black and male
i will not let
you slip through
the school system
which acts as if
you are unteachable

so tell them
tell them
you have you a mother
who remembers
all the fears
all the pain
all the discomfort
she endured in getting

*(Continued)*     59

you here
and she will not give you up
will not give you up
to no one
but the love of life
and to help shape
the dreams
of our people

tell them
tell them
now

— OPAL PALMER ADISA

# Sisterlove 1

Hug your brother, little sister,
hug him hard.
Kiss away his tears and
bring back his smile,

'Cause in the springtime of his manhood,
he'll laugh at your attempts at affection;
he'll be too busy proving his "manhood"
to let his brotherlove show.

Hug your brother, little sister,
hug him long.
Tell him stories of our people
and help to ease his way.

'Cause in the chill of the world
he'll be challenged every step he takes
he'll be tested every day
he won't have time to let his brotherlove show.

Hug your brother, little sister,
hug him strong.

'Cause in the winter of his disillusion
when he's grown too big, too distant,
too bitter for you to comfort, you'll
know that it's not all his fault.

—JOHARI MAHASIN RASHAD

# For Uri at 16

Though your stretching toward manhood
    has not been without pain—
    father gone, mother tired—
You have risen, a golden presence
    in your midst.

You know the Good,
recognize the Madness,
and move through them both,
floating on your broad smile,
confidence stored in your strong back.

Your eyes flash insight into a world
    we will not know.
You engage the difficult as readily as the easy,
    not baffled by mechanical complexity or
    friends' confusion.
We have watched you recover from intermittent
    fumbles with an athlete's courage;
    observed you dance with fervor,
    caught the first glimpses of your youthful
    wisdom.

Fourth generation son of Africa,
You give life to many ancestral shades.
They swing happily forward
    on the energy of your long stride.

— ANEB KGOSITSILE (GLORIA HOUSE)

# To Kyasa, Little Brother

Sometimes we can find
no reflection of the light,
fear to have lost our way,
doubt our tortured planting at dawn
will ever bear fruit.
We stagger in the violet hour,
wish for a hand extended from the shadows.
We cannot see ourselves,
or the road beneath us
in this fog.
But little brothers see
where older eyes grope,
dance behind us on the path,
feet sure where ours find sliding stones.

For this dance of faith, we thank them,
and walk with new confidence.

— ANEB KGOSITSILE (GLORIA HOUSE)

*October 9, 1983*

# young blood

You with your
african medallion
kente cap
walking tall
feeling good
about self
your eyes
on tomorrow

you will not see
yourself on television
you will not see
yourself on billboards
chest out
no dope
in your veins
you no hustler
or seventh grade drop-out
you read malcolm x    garvey    dubois
you get high off wynton marsalis
anita baker    public enemy
your eyes
on tomorrow

when you pass
me in the streets
you greet me
sister
nod your head
in respect
your smile
full and confident

in school
you're ignored
or told
you have a chip
on your shoulder
because you refuse
to be boxed in

you don't act all loud
or play like you bad
you listen
sort out details
strive for knowledge
your eyes
on tomorrow

hey young blood
brother/son
keep on steppin
you shinin for
all of us
we chantin
for all of you


— OPAL PALMER ADISA

# Nephews

When these tall black men
waltz smiling into my livingroom
I recollect toddlers in high tops,
missing front teeth now all turned
into muscle and low octaves
that are knowledgeable of engines
and cross-country driving.
Occasionally, though I would never
say as much aloud, I see a trace
of baby dimples and hear
the delicate gurgle of crib laughter
after a good tickle.

— STELLA L. CREWS

# From Father to Son

*(for vinnie, tarik, & in memory of philip farrar)*

it's no surprise
you are
the man you are
proud
determined

black men
have had
rough roads
to travel
and a hard path
to place their feet
but your grandfather
a cripple with two wooden
legs walked strong with a cane
and reared his son
to stand up
showed him
that feet
were the heart
and will the director
he carried a gun
and took no crap
from anyone
and when those
white boys
tried to run him over
tried to tell him
he was nothing
he took out his pistol
and shot out their tires
because he knew
the ground on which he stood
and your father understood
responsibility    respect    family
and you saw him being man

*(Continued)*    67

and you grew into manhood
knowing black men
have steep roads to walk
but their feet are in their hearts
and they still walking
just like your grandfather

— OPAL PALMER ADISA

# Four Poems for Gordon

*I. South Paw Baby*
  (at age six months)

I tried to make you right-handed soon,
But you couldn't find your mouth with the spoon.


*II. Black Diamond*
  (at age fifteen)

The kids are practicing rock —
"BLACK DIAMOND" they call
themselves     My living room
comes alive

How do I describe the sounds
that I hear?   Voices,
laughter, music, drums,
a medley caught in the trauma
of life

a waiting
a dividing of space
a reaching for the longitude
        wantonly pulling the poles
        that measure the ends
        of earth

Their private hells suspended . . .


*III. Gordon*
  (at age twenty-one)

            Now
a man     His jazz
a flight to magic
soaring with a downbeat
progressive, cool, funky

*(Continued)*

His appearance conservative
This boy four generations away
from slaves of the dormant
fields

His drums
beat a vocal message
He "gigs" his way into
his own world and circles
angels, devils, with African
telecommunications in this
modern idiom

Gordon, my manchild,
grown to mid-proportions —
his silences tracking the
dawn


*IV. Rite of Passage*
(at age twenty-one and a half, moving away
from home into his own apartment)

Moving up, out, into
your own orbit
you tell me about Steinbeck's
"Flight"— and you quote
"rite of passage"
What is that, I ask

You say it is the "right"
to move into your own,
to define your own space,
to grow into the sunlight
of your own cranial sphere,
the shadow of your
walk through time
and music
Your own sadness —
to measure that distance —
your own dance


70

articulated with the drumbeat
of your heart

rite of passage — we
each have as a legacy
of growing up and daring
to challenge the terrible
beauty of our own alienation
our own walk in space
our own weightlessness
in a world of spiralling
centrifugal force — a race
to the unknown

a rite of passage


— PINKIE GORDON LANE

# For My Brother

my last swim
and final push into this whiteness

your bright roundness
peering through narrow wooden bars
your hand reaching in
to squeeze me out for play
marks the beginning of me

in separation
you are snapshots
leaning over birthday cakes
and fishing rods
you are choruses
miracles
summertime
limes
applesauce
biscuits and froglegs
you are mother     father
gone

the words you spoke
calling me to share your place?
i want to speak them
so you can come home.

— MONIFA ATUNGAYE

# My Brother's Hand

There was a tree.
Trustingly, he clutched a limb
as he scattered downhill
to break the fall (yet to keep

the running). Down. Down.
When he reached the bottom,
he noticed that his hand
had scattered, too,

wrenched, ripped, opened,
blood he did not feel,
pain he could not scream,
shape he could not remember.

That was in Korea.

Before that (as a child)
the dog, vicious, snarling,
hungering badly for that hand
as it reached for a baseball

in the animal's yard, the hand
between the wired fence
that said, KEEP OUT.
(He never knew how.)

Then the machine that watched
him coming, binding books
at the Pentagon, keeping
the holds sure for all

of those military meals likely
to be served within the hour,
so the machine ate (why not?)
one-fourth of a finger.

He worried about the scar.

Lately, the trash bin
holding a small horror:
jagged glass in a plastic sack.
Everything waiting, including

the next blood, the next pain,
the next mutation, the next
assassination of his grasp,
the clutching, the reaching,

the binding, the bringing,
a journey of a hand,
of what is hungry,
what ravishes.

— DOLORES KENDRICK

# To Darnell and Johnny
(February 23, 1973)

*Owen Darnell Winfield, born May 22, 1945, and John Percy Boyd, Jr., born January 2, 1949, were assassinated by an agent of the state for struggling for Black liberation.*

I will always remember
how much life
is you.
your smiles
could cure with bright
stars of laughter.

I will always remember
how much life
is you.
your strength
could hug and protect
with peace-giving arms.

I will always remember
how.much love
is your life.
giving them for
tomorrow's children
of the universe.

I will always remember,
and you will always live
in the Spirit of the New World
you helped to build.

—MELBA JOYCE BOYD

# October Lament
### (For Clarence)

Frame angular, skeleton
leaning toward death
gushing dark waves of bile

Face carved
in ebony pain, teeth jumbled
in familial design

Pattern of generations
persistent still in timbre
of God's chosen voice . . . . . . .

*In open Bible, futile*
*passages of hope highlighted*
*green in lifeless hands* . . . . . . .

Outside the leaves dance scarlet
and gold. They sizzle in celebrations
of flame on rain-glanced pavement

But Brother, your stillness
hovers over me this crystal day
like premature icicles

melting their chill
upon my wilted spirit
drop by mournful drop

— NAOMI LONG MADGETT

# III

## *Lovers*

don't know why
they say you don't
exist cause i be
seein you
all the time . . . .
*(Opal Palmer Adisa)*

"a man of black satin
rustling in my night . . . "
*(Collette Armstead)*

# A Song of Praise
## for the Often Overlooked Men
*(for neville & karl)*

don't know why
they don't see you
cause you always
been there
been around
doing the same thing
for your woman
your children
your friends
the community

you man
deep chocolate
you man
sandy brown
you man
yellow
you man
nutmeg
you always been there
i've seen you
child raised
on your shoulder
i've seen you
apron round
your waist
cooking up a storm
i've seen you
bending
in your garden
your hands yielding
vegetables to nourish
i've seen you
tickling your wife
laughing into her

*(Continued)*

eyes being faithful
working every day
sometimes two jobs

don't know why
they say you don't
exist cause i be
seeing you
all the time
all over the place
doing the same thing
being a real good man

— OPAL PALMER ADISA

# You Are Like the Coming of Dawn

You are like the coming of dawn.
Refreshing.
You touch the withered stalks
of yesterday's *malaise*,
cast a tender manlet
over the hopes of today.
Swiftly passing,
but sometimes
a faint blush lingers

— IRMA McCLAURIN

# Sam

You gave me morning
birds singing *a cappella*
smell of country air in the city
visions of peace

No one
could draw me into their pain anymore
color me blue
or
paint sad pictures in my image

cause, YOU GAVE ME MORNING

I would never
wait by another window
cry all night
or
subdue my laughter
again

You introduced me to candlelight breakfast
champagne toast
and early day loving

Didn't matter how often

clouds hovered
pain knocked
or
suns set

CAUSE
sitting there
all toasty colored
sunny side up, full of honey, offering me your juice

man
YOU GAVE ME MORNING

— BEVERLY JARRETT

# For Yellow Roses

*For green lilies, white lilies, yellow roses,*
*the right to call it as you see it and the*
*responsibility to create it as you wish it to be.*

a black swan
gliding on reflective waters

a man unruffled
as black silk

a man of black satin
rustling in my night

a man
who hears
the dream covered scream

a man
who sends
yellow roses in the midst of winter

— COLLETTE ARMSTEAD

## what i love

you
rolling your eyes over ill-timed jokes, you
frowning over humanity's unending problems.  you
whispering secrets to our daughter.  you
muskperfuming my evenings.  you
planting summer gardens.  you
harvesting autumn love.

— DEVORAH MAJOR

## For Leonard
### in Our Twentieth Year

Each
day with
you is like
the restful shade
a great oak tree gives.
You are cool meadows when
rain has fallen. You are my
constancy, my haven from storm.

—NAOMI LONG MADGETT

# Song for My Beloved

My lover has sloe eyes . . .
that shine in the sweet
afterglow when lovemaking
is done

and a voice as smooth
as the rustle of silk
soothing as the sea,
honey-tinged tones,
slow, slurred and soft
laced with a down home melody

Son of the South
Odie Sr. and Elzada's firstborn
blessed with a tender heart
and a mighty spirit

Strong hands,
steady gait
simmering sexuality

Revel in his touch
rejoice in his presence
welcome the smile
that lights a flame
inside my soul

Each morn before daylight
streaks the sky
let me see the sun rise
in my lover's sloe eyes.

— ERICA ANNETTE PIERCE

# As I Recount My Love

When you enter the house, I listen
and I hear your slow but sturdy footsteps
as you climb and wind the stairs.
It's then I feel a prop behind me,
firm as a hardy oak.
Then when you have mounted to the top,
you come jauntily upon me
and, in proudness of me,
kiss me on each cheek
with your peppermint breath,
and stroke very gently
the contours of my sides.

Glad when night folds in upon us,
I snuggle up to you
no matter the weather.
Early matrimonial days
interlace my thoughts . . .
In utter bliss, I sleep serenely.

— NAOMI F. FAUST

# Black Satin Stallion

black satin stallion
midnight pearl
onyx jewel
you . . .
seductive masculinity
sweet dark chocolate butta'
we've met before
i remember warmth
beneath deep brows
i know cool shadows rest
inside soft brown eyes
there
under shade of stolen desire
we met
  every crease
    every crevasse
thick full lips
exploring love
  you . . .
    me . . .
      us . . .
melting beneath
  curly
    kinked
      nappy
black hair
and loving it all
loving you
essence of manhood
loving you
warrior thru time
i remember loving you
black satin stallion
midnight pearl
  onyx jewel
    you . . .

      — PHAVIA  KUJICHAGULIA.

# On the Edges

How those ink-colored
dungarees
hug your thighs
Strong & Mighty
a lover's quarrel
explodes
into an unraveling
of passions
that crave
"touch-me-now" palpitations
only
to be quenched
w/insatiable aches
of fierce, unrestrained
erotica
on the edges
of a minute

— KAREN HALLIBURTON

# Love Dreadlocked

**I.**
Because you are truly "monumental"
not your hair
you
truly
monumental
I must look for your
mundane
features
and fasten my desire
tenaciously there—
remember you yanking the obstinate
zipper in your jacket,
remember your dry scratching
after sleep or satiety,
sucking your teeth
after scrambled eggs
fried hard —
yes, hold to the ordinary
in you to keep love real
or be carried away
in your ideal,
sometimes fierce,
always powerful, primeval.
truly
monumental
you, not just
your hair,
though its greatness
is
beyond
words.

**II.**
Are hours 24 where you live?
Does the day begin at 7, 9, noon
or sunset?
Are telephones nearby, like
on the end-table there

or on the floor next to your foot
or near the baby's toy?
No, you will say,
the hours are grey and numberless
when music's rhythm halts
and the stage collapses again
into unending weariness;
and phones are for people
who have something to say.
Do you really understand me
as well as you seem to?

## III.
And certainly you know
I am one —
body-heart-soul,
all of which I have given.
Certainly you have observed
all openings yielding
to your entering
heard the ah's in soft chorus
responding·
to the rhythms you set
ah, yes.
certainly you know
Yes, you know
certainly.


— ANEB KGOSITSILE (GLORIA HOUSE)

# Before Making Love

I move my hands over your face,
closing my eyes, as if blind;
the cheek bones, broadly spaced,
the wide thick nostrils of the African,
the forehead whose bones push
at both sides as if the horns
of fallen angels lie just under,
the chin that juts forward with pride.
I think of the delicate skull of the Taung child —
earliest of human beings
emerged from darkness — whose geometry
brings word of a small town of dignity
that all the bloody kingdoms rest on.

— TOI DERRICOTTE

[The Taung child is a fossil, a juvenile *Australopithecus
africanus,* from Taung, South Africa, two million years old.]

# Desert

Shadows dance along the wall
to the rhythm of our lovemaking.

African man, whose skin
is sometimes darker than the shadows,
shines gold with sweat,
a king lost in time.
I lie naked in the Sahara
waiting for the rain to come.

—KARLA FRANCESCA BRUNDAGE

# Romance

something about you
excites and entices me
i don't know what it is
but i am totally infatuated with you
impatiently waiting for a glimpse
of you
i long for you
dream
of having you
submit to
this obsession of
     wanting
         tasting
             loving
                 you
waiting
    wishing
        guessing
            about
sweet black cornbread you
black-eye-peas-n-beans you
i want to squeeze thru
the gap of your teeth
to nestle in the naps
of your hair
i want to care
for you
&
you
for me

awww baby . . .
my heart bleeds for you
every bone in my body
craves you
and i
alone
can harness this
unspoken passion
alone

ohhh baby . . .
engulf me
        kiss me
                lick me
with songs
that sing of love
no longer satisfied
with fantasies
of you
and eyes
that cry limpid pools
of babylonian warriors past
from the first
to the last
now you

ummm baby . . .
now you


— PHAVIA KUJICHAGULIA

# Seeking a More Private Word
*(for tarik)*

**I.**
the word love
doesn't begin
to articulate
what i'm feeling
doesn't begin
to define
how you make
me feel
doesn't
do justice
to you
african black man
striving
to live your word
struggling
to protect your children
working diligently
to keep ahead
of the bills
researching
to infuse your
students with
factual pride
about our history

i'm talking about
you
and i'm left
to resort to clichés
you — the startling
yellow-orange tongue
of a lizard
you — the open-fanned
tail of the peacock
you the clear flow
of the waterfall
you — a sweet mango
juices trickling down

the chin
i'm talking about
you
how you make me feel

## II.
if i haven't
said it already
then forgive me
i was too full
of the feeling
to say it
too afraid
if i voiced it
it would cease to be
but you insisting
on accompanying me
each time i went
to my pre-natal visit
meant everything
and more

what would
i have done
without you
when labor started
and the contractions
wrung my body
like a piece of cloth
trapped by a fan
you were there
to hold me
to help me breathe
to allow me
to abandon all bravado
and fall apart
on you

words should have
colors and textures
words should emit
smell and invite taste

*(Continued)*

words should explode
like fire-works
then perhaps i could
begin to make you
understand
what you have come
to mean to me
how much i am depending
on you being here
with me
with our children
you
african black man
are the meaning
of endurance
you *is* black gold


—OPAL PALMER ADISA

# Peaches

Your Georgia peachtree accent
dangles from the ends of a word
like ripe fruit I try to taste
on the branches of your tongue.

I swallow your lies because
they are sweet like peach juice
and they run longer than the Mississippi River
(like the lies told as truths to our unknown ancestors
on the peach plantations)
into the stream of my blood.

Words from our history
I unconsciously devour
as we park at the riverside
and listen to the hum of crickets.

With you there is always sunset,
always candy colored sky.
Peach flavored clouds float by
and surround me with the lies
I want to believe because they tell me
that you love me, love that makes you
beautiful. For the slaves of love,
what is false is safe.

Your peach colored love
is like a water color faded,
so I will sit with you
while my heart races in the windy
heat of summer
longing on the Mississippi
for more fruit to eat.

— KARLA FRANCESCA BRUNDAGE

# For the One

sometimes we never notice
a good man behind
thick glasses
soft-spoken
heavily sweatered    overcoated
reading a newspaper
or a book quietly

a man who politely
offers his hand

a man who always
asks for permission

because it no doubt means
he is:      a) too quiet
            b) too nerdy
            c) too nice
            d) all of the above

or what?
            a) not hip enough
            b) not the type of man
                    other women
                    would envy

& besides we say
'all black men
are no damn good'

so we never really
notice
      our no expectation
      our looking through
the jewel

searching for *the one*

— JENNIFER E. SMITH

# IV

## *Street Scene*

"my brothers clap their hands . . . . "
*(Pearl Cleage)*

"all of you are sculpture in motion"
*(Beth Brown Preston)*

# Summer Is Coming

the laughter in the street gets louder.
summer is coming
and my brothers clap their hands
and slap their hands
in front of the pool room/cool room/fool room.
summer is coming,
hours filled
with sideways walking
and dreams of naked, perfect women.
the laughter is a constant shout.
heads thrown back
and teeth grinning
in startled white evenness
from the face that always watches . . .
but summer is coming!
hot enough to make you shine
hot enough to heat the wine,
down inside that plain brown bag,
passing like a hoodoo charm
from hand to hand to hand.
summer is coming,
and my brothers whistle
and sway and say, "hey, baybee!"
as we pass by, pretending
we don't see them on this very same corner
at this very same time
every single day, but hey,
summer is coming,
and my brothers
clap their hands.

—PEARL CLEAGE

# Harry's Afro Hut

Harry's Afro Hut in Baltimo'
Where the brothers can be brothers
No shootin' and buttin' heads
Brothers be talkin' sharin' and
Bondin' instead
Shorin' up their manhood against
The bullshit outside the door
That for lesser men could kill
The life spirit inside
From miles around and across the state
They come in droves to escape from
The daily emasculation of whitey's hate
At Harry's the facade comes off like
The brothers' drawers on a red hot date
The transition is as smooth as the
Geometrical lines and fades they be gettin'
Mayors, doctors, po' and average brothers
Uneducated and intellectuals be sittin'
Side by side conversin' rightin' the
Wrongs of a world that would consume
Them and all the while the brothers be
Role modelin' for the little bros that's
Waitin' to have their "do" styled sleek
Proud and cool as they watch and listen
To the incomparable logic and strengths
Of the black man not seen or heard
On television 'cause of society's
Fear of revealing truths that would
Weaken The Man's unholy grasp on
The world if all were told
So I pray that Harry's Afro Hut
Like the Pyramids stands forever
With the barbers Berry, Malcolm
And Leroy shadowing tall as Pharaohs
Images of intellect, strength and

Beauty that cannot be wrenched from
The minds of generations to come!

That's Harry's Afro Hut
Where brothers come out
Fades tall and chests high
And the Revolution continues!

— LUCY E. THORNTON-BERRY

# Direction
(Political advice for young brothers)


It ain't no big thing.
It's like where you live, man,
and who lives there with you.
For example:
You from Harlem?
Yeah, well, couda been Johannesburg or Birmingham,
you know? It's all the same. I'm from Fillmore.
That's makes us brothers, man.
Like we grew up in the same family, you dig?
I mean, like if you get shaky
about who you are and where you're going,
ask somebody who lives near you,
cause that's where it's at, man!
They'll set you straight!
You can't just go and ask anybody, man,
cause, dig, they just don't know.
They ain't been where you go — everyday.
They ain't been through your neighborhood, man.
They can't give *you* no directions!


— ANEB KGOSITSILE (GLORIA HOUSE)

# Blue Lights in the Basement
(From "Motown Suite")


FLASHBACK! FLASHBACK! FLASHBACK!
in high school we used to say
"ain't nuthin' but a party!"
which meant nothing short of paradise.
stacks of the latest 45's clicking
into place on the record player,
a blue light for atmosphere
screwed into the socket over the wash tubs,
and when the slow records came on, no lights at all,
or a lock on the basement pantry door
for those who had moved beyond the simple pleasures
of grinding one fully clothed pelvis against another

"nuthin' but a party!"
and we would dance and drink wine
and hope the thugs did not arrive,
but when they did
(and they always did,
umbrellas that had nothing to do with rain
tapping in front as if they were blind men,
stingy-brim hats cocked in defiance of gravity,
or greasy do-rags wound, rewound
and tied in front, low over the eyes . . .)
when they did arrive,
we would walk, trancelike, into their arms,
letting them fold their hot, black leather coats
around us,
licking and whispering in our ears,
laughing and growling down deep in their throats,
moaning us into dim corners
until we, choking on our own delighted giggles,
leaned back to look into their eyes,
disapproving and prissy,
pressing our teasing virgin breasts
into their forbidden banlon chests
and wondering what possible sweetness life had to offer
that could be finer than this.

— PEARL CLEAGE


107

# The Clothes You Color

Man, you sure look good in that black!
It's enough to stir a poor girl's soul.
You do look good in that black;
make my blood run cold.
I stop dead in my tracks —
don't give nobody else no slack
cause when you wearing that black, you be
a show-stopping, bebopping, rag-mopping
hell of a speci-man.

Man, you sure look mean-mean in that black.
Can't concentrate on the goings-on.
You look so good in that black!
Don't mention my mind cause it's gone.
My feelings be ran-sacked cause
when you wearing that black you be
up-setting, go-getting, pace-setting
dyno-mite inspiration.

When you wearing that black, man, you innovate,
generate, create a most relaxing atmosphere
and that's a cool/groove, cause I know
where your head be.
But your heart be another matter,
a thing of mystery.

— (MALIKA) ODESSA DAVIS

108

# a poem of praise

*(for larry neal & the 13th & f sts. crew)*

hollywood is
    gold
    cash
    limo
    coke
    cultural assassins/
       & them sistahs
       the w h i t e  shade of brown
       you dig?
dark slicksters cruisin
lost souls sellin cheap/sellin out to
    synthesizer
    mixers
    videos
       (the all american white anglo audience
       submerged in negro dreams)
          can't burn no fire
          on you/young brothas
          magic flames/
          explode
          pulsate african rhythms/
          command buckets
          to do ritual dances
          with stick arms
          beat dark hearts
          in time to celebrate
          on a street corner
          echo
          yo own
          blacksicians
          flow
          yo rhythmic
          rivers

— JENNIFER E. SMITH

# I Am Willie or Amos . . .

I am Willie or Amos or anyone
Of 20 million sons of domestic workers and project dwellers,
Do-ragged children of the revolution,
Black turbans pulled tight,
Sporting wide striped sweaters and the grace of Italian shoes
Defying the fear-struck Sunday afternoon stares
Of the "great society" out for a stroll.

In my portable rhythm & blues world,
I am strong, smooth, sharp in the pawn shop window,
The ten cent store.

— ANEB KGOSITSILE (GLORIA HOUSE)

# all the brothers

all of you are sculpture in motion.
all my heart twirls like a top at one glance:
"hello, sister, you look as lovely as this day."
i see you when you're old and dignified
riding busses not complaining about injustices
older than you.
you rob a store you run for mayor.
our fate rides with you from ship of chains to cadillac,
but don't look back, only ahead.
you may be thrashed, but you still smile at your keeper.
your instincts are the loving ones that no prison can kill.
in your eyes, brother, i see all others.
the faithful will prosper in you and of you,
unafraid you father a new race, conceive our new beginning.
we'll burst forth into song  and ride
the chariot to higher ground.
we have graced the streets of unwholesome twilight.
now we will stride into the sunrise, my brothers.
your eyes are the eyes of history,
the eyes a woman like me can love.

—BETH BROWN PRESTON

# Just Love

Love, just Love
seeing my Brothers
RUN    JUMP    SHOOT
Bounce  Bounce
a performance
at a neighborhood park
tall, extra-tall, lean, slick
& short evenly put-together bodies
hopping around in high top Adidas
w/man/sweaty sweat socks
accentuating
well-rounded calves
leading up to well-developed
strong thighs,
& flat,
or maybe not-so-flat stomachs
enhanced by hanging
and hugging shorts
& clinging T-shirts
redefining/tantalizing
RUN    JUMP    SHOOT
Bounce  Bounce
Sweat, pouring
in multitudes of transparent beads
oooooozing down fine faces
legs traveling
liquefying at full speed
RUN    JUMP    SHOOT
Bounce    Bounce
Hey, little bit
ORANGE BRIGHTNESS
what do you do
Love, just Love

— KAREN HALLIBURTON

# curtis michael
*(For my brother)*

four boys, a girl & one wife
keep you moving dawn to darkness
one dog, two cats & three sisters
create a condition where no fat
dare grow. so animate, those blasts
at how the cities are run, cars built,
housing on the market. so wise
you are in the personal histories
of all the buddies you collect
& drink beer with on saturday.

you hold down two jobs, one ancient truck,
two like new cars & a mortgage. so
elaborate, these gestures of who cares
anyway or it is just some talk & nothing
to do about stress or other complaints.
hold on to one popcorn popper, four
hunting rifles, three turtle doves
and a whole bunch of chuck holes
in the parking lot.

— STELLA L. CREWS

# Beautiful Black Men
*(With compliments and apologies
to all not mentioned by name)*

i wanta say just gotta say something
bout those beautiful beautiful beautiful outasight
black men
with they afros
walking down the street
is the same ol danger
but a brand new pleasure

sitting on stoops, in bars, going to offices
running numbers, watching for their whores
preaching in churches, driving their hogs
walking their dogs, winking at me
in their fire red, lime green, burnt orange
royal blue tight tight pants that hug
what i like to hug

jerry butler, wilson pickett, the impressions
temptations, mighty mighty sly
don't have to do anything but walk
on stage
and i scream and stamp and shout
see new breed men in breed alls
dashiki suits with shirts that match
the lining that complements the ties
that smile at the sandals
where dirty toes peek at me
and i scream and stamp and shout
for more beautiful beautiful beautiful
black men with outasight afros

— NIKKI GIOVANNI

# Afrikan Poet, Arise

African griot
Disguised by the American ghetto
Afrikan warrior
Winning with wit and wisdom
Senegalese soother
Saturated in the singleness of S. E.
Nubian Nimrod
Knocking off narcissistic oppressors
     At pen point
Bantu born Beninian
Boxing Bothas on both sides of the Atlantic
Ebony Egyptian,
Eliminating educated ignorance
Kenyan Kenny Carol
     Cloistered in a contrite
     Contemptible country
     Contemplating his connection
To the ethereal ancestors
Allegiance to Afrika

—WANDA WINBUSH

a short poem for righteous brothas
because you are:

afrikan sundancers.

warriors without spear
or crown.

stormbearers in unholy
land.

flames of survival/
patriotical line.

mystic men.

black magicians.

— JENNIFER E. SMITH

# Never on Prime Time

My man won't be
Seen on television
Showing his prowess
As a lover
Caressing breasts
And licking necks
And rendering
A woman weak
No my man won't be
Seen on television
In all of his glorious
Manliness 'cause
The Good Ol' Boys'
Women wouldn't want
*Them* any more.


— LUCY E. THORNTON-BERRY

# Who's Really Got the Power?

Brother you wanna know
Why white motherfuckers
Try to keep you from living?
'Cause you wave your thang
Like its the goddamn flag of
The USA, and it stands erect
Against the winds and storms
Of their sick obsession and
Secret love of your phallus
That with each pull of your
Trigger you turn the stars of
The red white and blue to
Glorious black!

— LUCY E. THORNTON-BERRY

# V

## *Beacons*

"how we are nourished by
his every word!
*(Naomi Long Madgett)*

"the prophet no die
the prophet alive"
*(Linda Cousins)*

# Nat Turner

this feelin is limestone
burrowed in the earth

you see

you are still in our blood
            our veins
        wear your scars
for robes of silk

cuz you was almost there
and we followed you
into the swamps to meditate
and feast on wild birds

we followed you
and stuffed our mouths
with blackberries & cattail roots
            & pure water
        from secret waterfalls
        only you knew of

we followed you
        we played the fiddle
            &
        cut the pigeonwing
we listened
as you listened to the wind


        Ahhh! ——————— this was freedom

        lovin life and death
        as the same root
        of the weeping willow

who cares
    what happens
        when the wind
            blows

*(Continued)*          121

so freely
   thru your soul
     this way

— NUBIA KAI

# Commitment 2

Paul Robeson stood out in his passport
a committee of one
a committee of one who covered
    a lot of territory
the territory of dedication
a dedication to the freedom of his people
I knew him in that way
as a prominent artist
complete with talent with democratic ideas
    and revolutionary gestures
Never never holding back
Never never backing down
Never never selling out
    Projecting the story of dignity and love
    instead of the story of greed and corruption

And I want to be warm like him
funloving like him    creative like him
unselfish like him
with his kind of awareness
his kind of generosity his
kind of critical understanding
kind of strength    kind of vision kind of energy
kind of power kind of spirit kind of courage
kind of sensitivity yes
    Never never never holding back
    never never never backing down
    never never never selling out
Always projecting the story of dignity & love
instead of the story of greed and corruption

I knew him in that way
in the way of the spirituals I love
even though he didn't sing in the style
of my choice
But what does style have to do with commitment
After all contributions go beyond songs
    & I liked his baritone bass speaking and
    booming out in artistic brilliance
A protest against hatred and fascism

*(Continued)*    

A protest against racism and oppression
A protest against terror and fear
His song was an intense song of ancestral memories
His song was a song of faith and resistance
His song was a song of hope and creativity
Always making connections
Always being progressive
Always trying to live the life of struggle & determination
instead of the life of glitter and degradation
and I like that
the fact he could interpret the symbol
that his photograph had become
A powerful force significant to masses of people
I understood him in that way
as a person complete with confidence
                    and political intent
Never holding back
never backing down
never selling out

Projecting the story of dignity and love instead of
the story of fame and corruption
I knew him in those ways
                and I like that
                Never never holding back
                never never backing down
                never never selling out


— JAYNE CORTEZ

# Alain LeRoy Locke
(Teacher of Aesthetics)


He has gone from the tower,
one who led others in the climb
to realize tall spaces.
He spoke of truth and beauty
as if walking with companions.
Once looking beyond young faces
to the campus green with spring
he returned to smaller stature
sharing with gaping students awe
of phenomena of season and being.

His casual mention of Leonardo da Vinci's
left-hand angel and the Artist's dream
of helicopter wings and submarines
stunned us awake to our ignorance.
Side by side with Michelangelo
he seemed to hang from
the Great Cathedral dome
to will humanity an ageless renaissance.

We shared with him a flow of knowledge
drowning sometimes in his esoteric phrase
as clipped words polished Benin bronze
to a glowing heritage.
Responding to new imagery and impulse
we probed the dark world origin
of the Picasso riddle and romped
in a bacchanal of our own.

Recalling now we fit his tenets
to nuances, the rationale of living
only half-sensed in the early day.
Though late, we reassess the life
he assigned the abstract,
the continuum of reason he believed to be.
So remembering, we vision the tower
urged by echoes of a learned man.

— MAY MILLER

125

## Martin

his voice was
mountains —
rivers rolling
through tears
of blood as
hatred took
a backseat
to the love
which alone
can save
us all.

— ROXANNE WHITAKER

# Martin Luther King

Martin Luther King, Jr.
Pilot of humanity.
Precursor.
God-sent herald.

He was a vibrant King,
fleet of wit and fair.
His rich, ripe words of eloquent tone
leaped in resonance from his tongue.
He charmed an admiring world.

Martin Luther King.
He was ablaze with warmth and love;
he was a symbol of hope and justice
for the darker race;
he was a beacon of trust for the poor, suppressed.

He was natural, as a spring,
pouring out himself for noble Cause.
He exuded freely into endless streams —
self-giving and self-denying.

Martin Luther King.
God-revering!
He was a radiant light of the world,
vigorously protesting wrong —
yet not in violence.
He was honestly brave and respected —
yet humble and not puffed up.
He sought neither fame nor fortune —
but yet he was adorned with fame.

We saw him as a mammoth leader.
He labored to deliver his black people
to a land of basic freedom:
a land where seats aren't set or claimed by color,
a country where water is neither white nor black,
a nation where votes are weighed alike
for persons of every rank and hue.

*(Continued)*

We sensed how much he cared.
He cared for faces writhed in hunger;
he cared for gusty, able people
with meager jobs — or none;
he cared for lowly dwellers
in homes that cried D-E-C-A-Y.
He gave his heart to these.

We knew his visions.
He had honest dreams of freedom.
He dreamed of a nation
where all men are free —
to learn, to work, to live
to the mount of their reach.
He dreamed of peace among mankind.
He dreamed of people's walking together —
with hands clasped:
white people, black people
yellow people, red people
people of all races, all nations —
all people.

We know the love he left:
for Coretta,
who stood as firm by his side
as a strong noon-day sun;
for their jeweled prize —
Yolanda, Martin III, Dexter, and Bernice;
for steadfast kin, friends, and fellow workers;
for people, all people
scattered over the globe.
A great Almighty Force had a plan —
He had His plan for Martin.

Silenced now . . .
We have strong memory of him.
We know that nations shall remember him
in clear, clarion beat —
as years pile and file upon years.
Annals of history shall hail him blessed
for the gifts to freedom he bore.
They shall call him the B-L-E-S-S-E-D Martyred King.

—NAOMI F. FAUST

128

# little mecca

*(for malcolm x)*

> Thank God prophets fall
> more often on the back
> more often arms wide open
> more often
> the belly facing the sky!
>
> *(Tchicaya U Tam'si)*


'sweet honey, shut dat door'
lamentations rise
like ash-colored birds over little mecca
sunset ran scarlet as if
the star was bled by wind.
sand of Jeddah
    oases of the Nejd
rose the songs of exotic birds
from the desert's lap.
he dipped forehead to black stone
"I am the man you think you are . . ."
dippd to the black stone & died
haughty as shaka

The shoeshine man
cops & sips his syrupy tokay.
Furnace of an armpit
 pressd 'gainst the bar;
wine-skin belly
 spoof of his trousers.
'de young bessie smith on kater st . . .'
splashd in je reviens . . . $20/bottle
bessie the nightingale
    wrapped in blue velvet
cood her restless tune.
Th amber wine retreats
to the bottom of his glass &
sweet honey rises, drops one
puppy's kiss for the ladies,
stumbles into shadows black

*(Continued)*    129

as a ruby's heart.
sweet honey moves on out the door.

Who believes in the unseen & the last day . . .
iron-facd in ethiopia
Observes prayer . . .
chantd in algeria
Pays the zakat . . .
sweet righteousness from omaha
Has Our blessing.
LA ILLAHA ILLA ALLAH
MOHAMMED AR RASUL ALLAH.

History is an ageless whore
grown bitter witness to
the drama of her crimes;
belly swollen w/
doomed foeti.
Mourn khadija & betty
for souls dispersed in the galaxy
revolvin like dice in the path of comets.
'Sweet honey, shut dat door.'

Ragged hat clutched to his chest, shine
box in hand
                pisswallow of a man
lumbers easy under easy moonlight
down to the corner . . .


— BETH BROWN PRESTON

# Malcolm

Good men don't die
they stay around
and take root
    in a cotton tree
And this tree grows
in a field that is barren
But because it is proud
and firm and strong
its very presence inspires
the other sprouts to thrive
and become great trees also.

And when I speak to my children
of you, Malcolm, this is
what I will tell them:
that you wore glasses and had
a shortcropped beatnick beard
but you wasn't no beatnick
    even when you beat tricky Dick
    and old white St. Nick.

I will tell my children
these things: that you were
tall, a giant,
not an ugly giant
a beautiful giant
with sandy-red hair
and a boyish smile
and even a few freckles
I will tell them this,
and the legends will grow.

I will tell them how you
destroyed John Henry
when you told him he was an
Uncle Tom nigger for
working himself to death
for white folks who didn't
give a hoot about him.
And I will tell them when

*(Continued)*     131

you spoke how your voice
traveled all over the world.
I will tell them
how you raised the dead on
the statue of liberty's carcass
and lifted the motherland
with your hands and brought
her near to us.

Think they'll believe me,
Malcolm, when I tell them
that you made it rain for us
that you were the rain
that brought life
to us
       when we were
            dead . . . dead . . .
                dead as your father's
                burning flesh under a railroad track
                dead as the men who murdered him
                dead as your mother's mind went
                    when she saw him.

Shall I tell them
how your words quickened
with the force of lightning,
entered the holes in our heads
              and became seeds?

See how we have grown?
       in this barren wilderness of
       prairie and cactus and crushed
           Indian head skulls
See how we have grown?
          out of the bloody sea
          the stinking ships
          the cotton fields
See how we have grown?

out of the dusty earth
· on the wings of the bazz*
perched high in our branches

I will tell them you were
Prince Shabazz, son of Elijah
Luqman, Prophet Muhammad
descendant of the line of Abraham,
that you arose out of
a mountainless forest,
that you cleared a path
for us and taught us not
to fear the beasts that
roamed in its midst.

You said: yes, animals are
flesh and blood and can die
just as we die.

See how we have grown?
who didn't know the Aryan horn
was made of glass,
that we were dealing with
a child warrior
painting pictures on Sundiata's helmet.

See how we have grown?
who didn't know our
own fragile entrails
were overcooked chitterlins
till you showed us
men were not flesh
but light
born of Allah's morning.

And on the morning
of the Great Feast
on the singing hills
where you walked
you left this tune:

---

*Arabic word for *eagle*

*(Continued)*     133

"We will be free!
One day our people will be free!"

Free as the bazz
unharnessed from
the American dollar bill
and mounted on this hill.

I will tell them
and the legends will grow
like the shoots
around a cotton tree
they will grow in
these words:

>             that you were a hewer of stone
>             a welder of nations
>             a maker of men
>             a master of self
>             a man with the spirit of the sun
>             that you were
>             our teacher
>             our leader
>             our Prince
>       and we will love you,
>                   always
I will tell my children
these things
and they will listen
            Malcolm . . . Malcolm


— NUBIA KAI

# Malcolm X

against the bloody blue
sky
formed from fears
and fertilized with the
bones of Black people
who died arching
in agony —
i wave my words
i give my body
i hold my rifle.
whatever i have been
whatever i am today
i have remained
a man
a
Black
man
to the last.


— ROXANNE WHITAKER

# George Jackson

The newsboy hands us
his death
and smiling leaves us wondering
what to do with it.
We shift from foot to foot
old discontents,
as the careful comfort in our lives
flicks off the bullet
that found the soft spot
in his back.
Still, some vague thing
about freedom
makes us nervous to know
where he went.

He falls hard into our memory
of others gone
for something or nothing.
Righteous rebel, he was tracked to the heights
of his road
that bent dangerously proud.
Though his spirit rose through deliberate fires,
he couldn't escape the ones
who sent the bullet.
But even those who knew their jobs
so well
only got his flesh,
because they couldn't strike
the awakened worth of him.

And we, reading his blood,
we jerk on tenterhooks
for fear a trail of broken chains
may lead to us.
Servants of safety, we live in our skins.
Our chorus is, "He can afford to be free
who has nothing to lose.
But those who have jewels
must stay in the grace of thieves."
And so we pull a cover

over our weapon of will
and yield to forgetfulness of him
with already drying tears.

— JILL WITHERSPOON BOYER

# marley no die
*(to the spirit of Robert Nesta Marley)*

the prophet no die
the prophet alive
AfriCAN man
marley spirit
forever walk the land

rastafari never die
rasta message move on
through I and I
carrying Jah people
to irie ites
all through Jah day
all through Jah night

the prophet no die
the prophet alive
Jah, garvey, marley,
selassie I
all live
and the message
still live
that each one give:

stand up, AfriCAN
claim your rights
claim your land
rise up, rise up,
AfriCAN

rastafarI, never die
rasta message move on
through I and I
Bob Marley spirit
still in the land
giving Jah message
to all AfriCAN
singing Jah message
to all AfriCAN.

— LINDA COUSINS

138

## the league of defense
*for Atty. Kenneth V. Cockrell ('38-'89)*

when revolutionaries
are sent
the time to move
is meant.
there is no reproach
in manner,
no hesitation
in diction.
your style
engaged the elegance
of the gazelle.

against the rich
profiting from
our life imprisionment,
and their politicians
petitioning
for the narcotic
incarceration of generations
policed under
STRESS,
you argued
for the defense
for the resurrection
of soldiers
in the factories,
in the streets,
in the churches,
holding court
for the people
in one
long
breath.

but we know this
who love you
who thought with you
who triumphed with you

*(Continued)*

grieve from the gut.
we share the same camp
and kindle this dream
called freedom.

these tears
that cleave our mourning
inspire this fire.
we see you
convening in sweet smoke
with our brothers,
JOHN PERCY BOYD,
HAYWARD BROWN,
MARK "IBO" BETHUNE.
very near here,
in the next haven,
planning the league
of defense
for our revolutionary
spirits
before our sentence
is passed.

—MELBA JOYCE BOYD

# Walk Proud, My Brother

Walk proud, my
brother
your gait is strong
though the
steps
aren't steady
your head is clear
under the hair of
grey
Walk proud, my brother

There she is, take her
hand
as you took it years
before
Walk with her and
talk of life beyond that
door

Follow the path, reverse the
steps
you took to enter
that grave
Walk that road and
think of the path you
cleared

Walk proud, my
brother
your will is tall
though the
frame
is bent
your heart is right
beneath the winds of
time
Walk proud, my
brother —
Mandela.

—SIBYL R. COLLINS

# Mandala for Mandela

The brown earth cracks
      and shouts.
The wind chants a planetary salute.
Stars turn night to day.
Millions of hearts burst.
The toi-toi trotting of the young warriors
      sounds like thunder,
      convulsing the hills.
The world's wheels squeal, racing
    to the greeting circle.
We hold each other, crowding like
      shy, happy children
      to behold the WONDER:
      YOU BACK AMONG US.
The sky  s m i l e s.
Hello. Nelson.
AMANDLA!
Our arms ache to embrace you,
SURVIVOR OF SOLITUDE,
DARK SUN OF CERTITUDE,
FLESH AND BONE of Africans' deepest longings.
AMANDLA, AMANDLA!
Another son, who is the Word,
is home and dwelling with us.

        — ANEB KGOSITSILE (GLORIA HOUSE)

# Black Poet

*(In memory of Langston Hughes)*

How we are nourished by
his every word!
How we roll it around
in our mouths
like ripe fruit
wishing to savor it long,
digest it slowly
into our selves!

He has cut down our harps
from drooping willows
and handed them back to us
commanding us to sing.
Our blues voices
he has amplified into
anthems of praise,

gathered fragments
of our splintered dreams,
kneaded them together
in healing hands and cried,
"Be whole!"

Surely it is his
nimble fingers still
that teach us how
to harvest ripe figs
from thorn trees
that were supposed to die.

— NAOMI LONG MADGETT

# To Langston

I plunged into the rivers of your mind
I swam in the night with the faces of my people
The moon was vanilla and shimmered the water
I swallowed dark waves in a river of blackness
Under the moon I swam until weak with memory
My arms and mind became limp and numb
Under the drum-beat sky I crawled onshore
I sponged my body dry on satiny soil
and watched as the dawn dimmed
your hut in the distance
You remember Langston
The one you built long ago by the Congo
I heard the ancient voices sing     inside
and like a lullaby     they lured me
and lulled me until I swayed to sleep.

— REGINA B. JENNINGS

# On Witnessing the Receipt of an Honorary Degree by Sterling Brown

Although the chaos of those walls
Bore none of Pennsylvania's academic calm,
Cheers shaped his rise, and the trumpets
Blared too loudly their *hubris* in brass tones.
The bard stepped forward in his robes.
Far from slavery's fields and Reconstruction's roads
The themes of such poems: "Long Gone,"
"Break of Day," "Strong Men . . . ."
I held my place at the foot of the stage,
A disciple among leaders seeing strength
Embodied in one man who poured forth
The sweet libation of so much lyric:
"Southern Road" and "Old Lem . . . ."
*Swing dat hammer — hunh —*
*Steady, bo';*
*Swing dat hammer — hunh —*
*Steady, bo';*
*Ain't no rush, bebby,*
*Long ways to go.*

They say I am caught in the destruction of music,
Between rhythms spoken and unspoken
between rejoicing and sorrowing
between darkness and seduction
between rising and falling.

I ran from that room of brave listeners
Picked up the hammer of poetry,
And struck the anvil of symphonies,
Took my place in the Negro caravan
Behind the "Dean of Afro-American Letters."
*Swing dat hammer — hunh —*
*Steady, bo';*
*Swing dat hammer — hunh —*
*Steady, bo';*
*Ain't no rush, bebby,*
*Long ways to go.*

*(Continued)*     145

But let me describe the sweet exodus of sound
When no explanation matters. It is so desolate.
I am a rag doll thrown over a child's shoulder,
And those people I see still walking the Mississippi's banks,
Who have known themselves, their mud and flatboats,
Swirling eddies that sucked away their children.

They say I am caught in the destruction of music,
Between rhythms spoken and unspoken
between rejoicing and sorrowing
between darkness and seduction
between rising and falling.

*Swing dat hammer — hunh —*
*Steady, bo';*
*Swing dat hammer — hunh —*
*Steady, bo';*
*Ain't no rush, bebby,*
*Long ways to go.*

—BETH BROWN PRESTON

# Robert Hayden

He words elegance in agony.
A poet's heart, raw from
love, is mindful of art,
the terrible vision.
He pens the craft, faithful to
the illusive muse, submits to
her favors, is victor, forgives.

*"...What is Art? What is Life?"*

He must ignore the noise of
critics who constantly shake
paper fists; must contest
ignorance, the indifference of
hurt, of promises, of praise.

*"Pilot Oh Pilot Me."*

His kin denied, save the
heavy memories of beginnings —
the boy who was whipped,
cursed, but who would get
away to see the brightness of
Detroit's brown dancers,
hear the Empress of the Blues.

*"That gaiety Oh that gaiety I love."*

From boy to man, the mystery:
hard truths, never too far to be
captured, like jewels from a king.
He is the warrior astride a fresh
horse, furious, passionate,
taking the middle passage
down to Mississippi.

*"Do you remember Africa?"*

*(Continued)*  147

Oh don't give him that ancient
title. Poet Laureate is meaningless
here. You do not honor your
men of wisdom, America, but
put them on display, abuse them.

*"Oh light beheld as through
refracting tears."*

Rather, let him alone to
sense the wonder, find
peace from his poems.
He gives his gentle genius
as your hope. And like
the ageless bards of older worlds,
he will remain symbol of all
that is exquisite, human, prized.

*". . . lives fleshing his dream of
the beautiful, needful thing."*

— SYBIL KEIN

148

# For Robert Hayden

He extended to truths
and believed abide
and called to comrades,
those faltering in the run
(the hopeless and the doomed)
and to those who, gifted,
lighted their flares
at his larger flame.
He had known them all,
had lived their stories
(the defeats, the acclaim)
while tracking the path
to a high green garden
where honor etches
a crystalline goal:
love of all mankind and art.

— MAY MILLER

# Epitaph for Etheridge Knight

you lunged
at this square toed
beast.
this condor convexed
inside your chest
stared it straight
in the eye
and read
poetry.

this decree
to defy
the endless suicides,
the deaths and dyings
of addictions
with dope and drink
in the fields of
cigarette dreams
chasing you
into the streets
to steal from
mothers and elders
only to return
as the unborn
to unlove the
beautiful eyes
of your daughters
and future sons
riding bicycles
and portable radios
into the black
anger of America
into the confrontation
without armor
leaving them
bleeding like
ulcers at the altars
of patriotic citizens
cheering the T.V.

video war
after the football
scores of 100,000
human beings incinerating
on highways
of Iraq
off camera
out of focus
in the flat,
white light
colliding inside
aluminum
houses in
Indiana
of no Indians
or anything sacred
but the religion
of basketball
stealing the souls
of brothers
migrating to
Philly and Detroit
or other hip places
to rise on the
physics of
invisible air
above corporate
closets where tongues
are traded with
thieves who chained
your grandchildren
to Dutch slave ships
and sodomized them
to relieve the
boredom of the ocean
voyage with no
forwarding address
or postage
except in the
margins of
the library
where the academy

*(Continued)*

applauded absurdity
and complicated
the simple truth
beyond recognition
to avoid the amber
in your eyes
and your dismembered
voice repeating
in this spiral
of descent
like an answering
machine receiving
an obscene
phone call.

the Devil resented
this poetry
of resistance.
this insistence
to remain sane
when the rest
of you
went crazy
with escape.
this art of
resurrection,
rose above "the
blood and mud
and shit"
of memory
to sing your
belly songs
of love

— MELBA JOYCE BOYD

# For Haki

Teach
me
to be
a
poet
so that
I
may write
like
you:
about
what we let them
do to us
and our unborn
using words
madder 'n hell
burrowing into minds,
yet
spreading
gentle love
among
the people.

— SATIAFA (VIVIAN VERDELL GORDON)

# a call-to-action poem
### *for dennis brutus*

i watch you walk a funny kinda
weary can-never-get-tired walk
kick up a long soldiers stride
true to hard journeys/
hard living
i witness your hair wiry
bounce to beat of
        african drummmm
words fall like spears
from your lips a
poet's prayer/

i hear/i feel woes of
south africa/robben island/
england/america
echo in your voice
a cry of house arrest/torture
        screammmminnng
organize african peoples
ready arms/

believe in sun
believe in moon
believe in the core of earth
believe in black
believe in power

— JENNIFER E. SMITH

# Zakee*
## (or An Afrikan Poet Appreciates an Afrikan Poet)

fiery-eyed poet
of tender heart
gentle woodworker
resonantly voicing
poetic prophecies
translating the wine-soaked
pain of a street-dwelling
          desperado
into vivid images
for a people
to live/learn by

        poor uncle bud
        his life is a blues song
        poor uncle bud
        his life — an Afrikan symbol
        of a system hopelessly wrong

fiery-eyed-poet
tramping through
the liquid storm
vibrating voice raised
above the din of the rain
and Brooklyn Bridge traffic
reciting the wilderness cry
of Dr. King's ongoing
poignant dream

gentle poet
power-voiced potent prophet
southern son
telling the children
teaching both the old and young
as the elders have taught him
through the Spirit
and through the ages

---

*Zakee Nadir is a multi-talented performing poet in Brooklyn.

*(Continued)*     **155**

living and giving love
through his poems
living and giving beauty
through the beauty
of his ever-creative
Soul.

— LINDA COUSINS

# VI

## Music-Makers

" . . . takes you through this
mean ole world . . . . "

*(Sybil Kein)*

# Barbecue Bob Hicks

could cook up a
mess of sweet ribs
at the Buckhead
drive-in-stand
in 1927;
but when he dished
up the blues,
all you tasted was
grits and turnip greens.

*"I'm gonna tell you gal*
*like the gypsy tol the Jew;*
*If you don't want me — it's a*
*cinch I don't want you."*

— SYBIL KEIN

# herman

herman used to sing a gin song
dance intoxicated rhythms
keep time to phantom music
imbedded deep
within gravel
and lacing
concrete cracks

he'd shake & lower his head
purse pink lips
        puffed from liquor an
        whistle & mumble & sing
        "Don't break it got to put it away
        Don't break it got to put it away"

herman was a son
             a brother
                   an uncle

was a sailor
swabbed by white decks

hopped to orders barked
from mouths neath
jauntily worn white caps

assigned to "colored only" duty and
                  "colored only" pay
scuttled/
    by a segregated navy

he wun't no marble
he wun't no kind uh stone
he wun't nuthin
        but a man
        a diamond in the rough
     buried deep

witness to a million lies weighin heavy
                              on a single truth . . .
Æsop stolen out of Africa
transplanted in Greece . . .

lil Black boys
chasin tigers round sum trees
meltin em to butter
            quick as you please
a heritage twisted
like a pretzel maker's dough —

abandoned in an alien land
with sign posts to self-respect
            all pointin to *NO*  broke
            his man heart
scattered it like
so many bits and pieces
of forgotten dreams

he was a low moanin a
high beseechin a
song played in the wrong key
hittin B flat
missin C sharp              always out of reach
made fast friends with hard times
                        and stayed
                              forever
                              faithful

herman used to sing
a gin song
wink a silent secret
            in one's direction
flick heavy wrists into
                  thick finger snaps
shake his head
push a whistle through
            his tongue
      mumble untold memories and sing
            & whistle & mumble & sing

*(Continued)*      **161**

"Don't break it got to put it away
Don't break it got to put it away
Don't break it got to put it away

                        put it away
herman

used
   to
         sing

— A. WANJIKU H. REYNOLDS

# cousin george

cousin George
kept his piano
in a place full-up with
home-grown love beatin strong
in the heart of harvest's corn fresh
      with husk's silky traces
a place where carin grew vine-ripe-heavy with nourishin

he tuned it to sweet bean/string pea harmonies
borne from soil-rich garden orchestration and Lord
    he made a joyful noise a joyful noise

cousin George tickled ivories
with hands strengthened by victuals
stewed n' brewed on a wood-burnin stove

he pulled tender from the creases in his palms
patience from his callous-weary fingers n'
made a gift of grace to a child of want
taught her "mary's lamb" and made it feel concerto
imprinted boogie-woogie rainbows on this child
    and held her heart forever

he personified love in a world
too busy for magic of *pretend*
too worn for travel in *universe of child*
they shared a sumptuous soul in a barren land

she made laughter of his teeth and song of his tongue
she was cousin George's one sweet angel child

but time calls for change
its movements rearrange
leaving memory    a golden shimmer
    in gloomy wake of loss . . .

cousin George in a room above the stairs
lay low in a bed of illness where air
played a somber tune of dusky deep despair

*(Continued)*    **163**

although her face could make his shine
and her chatter could ease his mind
         her hands were too small
they couldn't wield the mighty wand
         of healing's power

death stood the helm of cousin George's fate
but it could never man his gift of grace
nor change the course of love that flowed
         from him to me
         his one sweet angel child

cousin George
kept his piano in a place full up with love
touched ivory board n' made it sing
imprinted boogie-woogie rainbows on this child

*"ma-ry had a lit-tle lamb / lit-tle lamb she had a
lit-tle lamb oh ah say / ma-ry had a lit-tle lamb
its fleece / its fleece / was buhlaack as coal"*

— A. WANJIKU H. REYNOLDS

# Uncle Gus

Gus would sit at his piano:
Oh, how he played his Ghost Rags!
(which were written by somebody else).

The piano jumped and swooned,
shimmied around the middle,
made fun of his fingers

that were too fat to hit all
the right notes at the right time.
Two keys together: one wrong,

one right, what did it matter?
Gus had his long, lonely singing
song, drifting through his rich

black body like his mother's
homemade molasses. He sat
proudly playing in his little

parlor for his family: his nieces,
nephews, mothers and sister
(his pa long gone, dead of alcohol

and debt), Gus himself, a borrower
of sorts, now and then a little
borrowing from all those devoted

women, his good lean body,
his high-stepping legs, all in
greystriped pants, his strong chest

breathing through the white, crisp
shirt and black tie, the gold tie-pin
with a dust of diamond glimmering

in the afternoon light, as he took
his best step toward the piano again.
Sitting more upright than the music,

*(Continued)*     **165**

Uncle Gus ragged the piano to tin-cup
begging, reached for the cool glass
of his mother's wine on the edge

of the piano, sipped, danced in his seat,
laughed at the goodness of his rhythms,
and dared the ghosts to come.

— DOLORES KENDRICK

# Drum Man

Brown skinbeat pounds your hot rhythms
Strong hands play on the tom toms
Rocksway moves as your body
Syncopates itself against the congas
Drumming hot rhythms as you play
Makes me jiggle
   dip
   move
Cry for more drummystery
Makes me pulsate to your rhythm
Till it snares me and holds me captive
As you play me into ecstasy

      —WANDA G. WINBUSH

# Leadbelly

was arrested for
hard, hard living
getting dog mad
and killing somebody.
He turned 20 years
of chain-gang labor
into many a song.
Sang: "Take This Hammer,"
"Cotton Fields at Home."
*Whooo, baby,*
*wish I'd never*
*seen your face;*
*sorry you ever*
*was born.*

— SYBIL KEIN

# Jelly Roll Morton

Winin' boy,
if you were mine,
I'd rock you in my
cradle of careless love —
true blue love,
and let you jass me
with your sporting house,
red gravy, diamond-studded,
gambling, hot Creole
rambling, down-town
ragtime blues.

Lord Jelly, Oh Mister Jazz King,
You salty dog.

—SYBIL KEIN

# Louie

Can send you
        flowers, my dear,
of memories
        when you and I
were in the old days:
        streetcars and Saturday nights,
red beans and rice
        and gumbo-yassssss!
With that old horn laying on my lips,
        I played it all,
sweetheart,
        just for you.
Tripling rainbows in blue and brass,
        holding them high notes —
Jass, Jass, Jass!
        (Oh Yeah)

—SYBIL KEIN

# Thots of Coltrane
### (While Listening to Africa)

John Coltrane
Traveled many
Routes on his
Magical train.

Saxophone riffs
Transversing
The unknowing
Souls of us.

Spurting sounds,
Moods, melodies,
Rhythms, thots,
Ideas, sensations.

John Coltrane
Traveled and
Left us
His life!

—KENYETTE ADRINE-ROBINSON

# Hendrix

BLACK
BEAUTIFUL
SHINING
star
a real
STAR
fallen
out of
the sky
churning
cosmic
original
SPARKS flying
everywhere
until caught fire
in their haste
to consume —
CONSUMED EVERYTHING
except the music.

—MAKETA GROVES

*Written for the twentieth anniversary of the death of Jimi Hendrix*
*November 25, 1990*
*San Francisco*

172

# B.B. King

"I know
people everywhere
got reason to sing the Blues."
And his guitar-voice
makes you a believer,
takes you through this
mean old world where
ain't nobody love you
but maybe your Mama,
and you want to close
your eyes, like he does
and wail:
*"Lord, I really, really
have paid my dues!"*

— SYBIL KEIN

# Max Roach / The Rhythm Wizard

One very special day
A long, long time ago
A lonely Drum-spirit fell in love
Fell hopelessly/hopefully in love
With a yet to be born Black/baby/man/child
She whispered irresistible rhythms
In the ears of his soul
In the warm night-like darkness of the womb
She shared her ageless secrets
Bathed him in the healing waters of the musical truth
Promised him unbelievable, but achievable powers
Teased him daily with dreams of greatness
Said, there is happiness in me
Magic melodies in me
Freedom-medicine in me
You'll find yourself in me
She said, I am the gift & the burden
I am your joy & your weapon
I am the internal thunder
That will make you strong
And keep you keeping on
I am your inescapable destiny
Your soul/your lover/your very being
I am your one & only reason to be born

Some folks choose to play drums
But Max surrendered to an ancient calling
And let the drums play him
Sway him . . . . . hypnotize him
Praise him . . . . . fight him
Protect him . . . . . guide him
Scold him . . . . . hold him
That jealous Drum-spirit loved him so much
She damn near worked him to death
Declared herself an uncontrollable obsession
And had him at his drums morning, noon & night
"Forever" depended on it!!!

Max Roach doesn't play at playing rhythms
Max Roach is rhythm

All rhythm/rhythm incarnate
The universal Rhythm-wizard
African rhythms/his biological alarm clock
Afro-American rhythms/the bounce in his walk
Afro-Brazilian rhythms/the strength of his laughter
Afro-Caribbean rhythms/the power of his anger
Afro-Latino rhythms/his lullaby
Even his tear-drops are syncopated

Some people choose to play drums
Max never had that choice
Max was introduced to his soul-mate
And the drum became his voice
When the drum said . . . . . Max,
I want to dance with you
Max danced
Still dances . . . . . always dances on his drums
When the drum said . . . . . Max,
I want to sing with you/thru you/in you
Max found the melody
Like he danced on those drums
Til they sang like a saxophone
Like a flute/like a bird/like a lover

One very special day
A long, long time ago
A lonely Black/baby/man/child fell in love
Sang a "hope to die"/gonna live forever love song
To an ancient love-sick Drum-spirit
I say, Max Roach was born
Into a musical marriage, pre-arranged by fate
And the universe will never be the same

— AVOTCJA

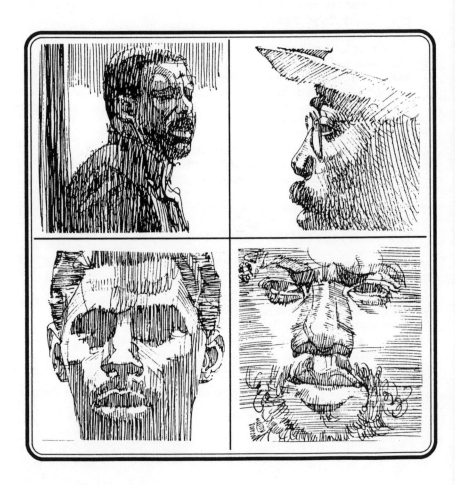

# VII

## In Light and Shadow

"he revives the spirit . . . "
*(Monifa Atungaye)*

"So many doors, knobs, rails!"
*(Toi Derricotte)*

# African Sunrunner

Run in warm sun
Bring legs up Kilimanjaro high
Down Nile River flow
Like mothers' milk
Come running to mouth
Nurture all

Run past Khemit
    past Mali
    past Ghana
    past Nigeria
    past colonialism
    past independence
    past internal strife
    past revolution
Back to the sun

— WANDA G. WINBUSH

# "The Sun Do Move"

Who wouldn't believe,
who wouldn't,
who wouldn't believe?

Camp meeting outside
the city limits.
Corn-high, the yellow wave
of faith, gushing
on his word.

    And God said . . . .
        *Preach it, brother!*
    The Good Book reads . . . .
        *Yes, it do, Lawd, it do!*
Day climbing over the southeast
corner of the earth,
grasping for the truth.
        *Tell it, John Jasper,*
        *Hallelujah!*
All day long, all Sunday afternoon
the fields outside of Richmond rocking.

Sun melting down like lard
on the griddle of the world,
the hungry square of earth swallowing
it up again.

        *Come, Jesus!*

Who wouldn't believe?
Who wouldn't, who
wouldn't believe!

— NAOMI LONG MADGETT

*(John Jasper [1812-1893 or 1901], a former slave, accepted the entire Bible literally and, through exhaustive study, was able to "prove" the mobility of the sun and the flatness of the earth. His famous sermon, "The Sun Do Move and the Earth Am Square," drew crowds of worshippers to his church, as well as to camp meetings in the country. So convincing was his sincerity and so powerful his oratory that even those who knew better were convinced, even if only momentarily, of the authenticity of his claim.)*

# The Blacksmith

In chambers filled with bluenote hieroglyphics
and portraits of astral travelers
he revives the spirits
ceremony from the book of the dead
he breathes and burning they dance
curving muscles and wings into grace
revived memories.

The fire breather
echoes of a coda  a code  a lode (star)
seep into brilliant frames
some moved beyond my real
there is too much magic
    not Robeson but his grandeur
    not Bird but his flight
and magic can erase pain
its absence awes
but doesn't touch me
yet
those twilight gods
sparkling
summon me to breathe fire and walk with them.

Complete breath.
Flame.
The laughter sounds.
Osiris, companion.
Isis, sister.
I hear my august lover playin sweet and blue
The ginger women lyricin and moanin low
Home cookin.
Mo greens, please.
Sated.
Yellow blue skies at setting
seeing you says everything is everything
just as i pray

I want to grow round like you
grow like the wild honeysuckle outside your door
witnessing your alchemy and
flowering in melting nights of love.

— MONIFA ATUNGAYE

181

# The Janitor (Circa 1940)
*(from "Saturday Night")*

Alone in the cellar
He stoked the furnace
Fire etching margins
Along the scroll of his day.
This night loud in liquor fantasy
With bared fangs of flame,
The hissing of steam,
He denied memories of that
Which cooled his youth:
>The tongues of new grass
>Lapping sunlight,
>Water running to meet water
>Where rocks round their edges.

For the blazing hour he was entity —
Furnace, flame, and steam —
His forked song raised
In identity with God:
>He wrestled with angels,
>Rescued God's children,
>Calmed the raging beasts
>In their den.

Then self (the insistent flesh again)
He loved and was loved,
Touched all the earth plàces,
Rode his dragon across the night.

— MAY MILLER

# Joe Louis
*on the occasion of his burial at Arlington Cemetery, April, 1981*

golden gloves melt on the hot sands
& the vultures wait for the white glint
of teeth handling white sheets
to join their feast
the desert is hot
& they are thirsty for hallucinatory peyote juice
so they can soar above a dead man
& ride the silver cloud of his hope
to claim his afterworld
where the thrones are not taken in sickness & age

he is gone
he is their boy now
the cameras flash over and over
taking snatches of his life
papers thick with his handprints
blow on the streets
he is their boy now
a memory in the sewers of time
the great white hope of charity checks
extinct in the unchallenged sun
they mourn with the false mornings that preclude dawn
tears thin as smoke trickles from their mouths
the cameras flash
& the vultures quench their thirst on the blood of bombs
& the vultures do psychedelic acrobatics on
                              Southwind windowsills
the vultures gloat frenzied acorns in their jaws
charmed by their murders
& the punching bag flesh of a King

the ceremony is ready
planes hustle from the broad face of forgotten wars
to shoot hurrahs into the sky
to shoot down stars
fireworks blast over an ocean of bones
trumpets play the circus of dignitaries
ropes barring his flock
look on out of cracked mirrors

*(Continued)*                      183

we do not know him in this way —
without the zoot suit smiles
       & softness of cotton bolls
Niger running gold thru our fingers . . . .
we are amazed that we have so little
     & yet so much
we are amazed that we have so much
     & yet so little
that the gold of our teeth
cannot be held by our hands

he is their boy now
the American dream
on the mortal bier of peace
brown bomber of German jellyrolls
ole Missus rescued again from yankee pants
the trumpets blow round table forests into snowflakes
Arlington is honored
he is dead now
the ideal warrior is dead
buried among the dead who were always ghosts
now roses will grow out of the mute earth
choked with evil
now towers will stand a little longer
to shoot lethal ink at sheep

we do not bleat
when the river bends another way
to feed the land
Joe goes with us
to the secret places of manhood
laughing at all the delusion in a silver coin

Arlington is honored
her perfumes drift to the moon
her gates open like the jewel of the lotus
to receive our King into their bellies
we are not fooled by the false mourning of mockingbirds
or the hidden rituals of unhooded knights
the round table turns
the chips roll down to the chicken coop

we are not fooled by the vulture's mask of bloody petticoats
he meant so much more to us then
a carnival of fallen saints
& pondwater on sloping chins
they see tragedies we do not see
except in the world he was born into
& when he said: "We will win because
                    God is on our side"
we heard djimbes & keelboats
& maul hammers destroying the steel forest
more than the gold of gloves woven in sand
the ultimate fate of tanks
                    we will win because
                water cannot be defeated
                        because
                a leaf trembles towards the sun
                        because
                the wind, impeded, howls
            & one cannot kill the deadly glance
                    of selflessness

he is their boy now
as his flesh to them was always
crisp brown American apple pie
we do not bleat
when the river bends another way
to feed the land

for us he lives
as the sea lives
in the gentle rain of warriors breaking rocks
for us he lives in the strength of a corn seed
for us he lives in the silent wind catching snakes.


— NUBIA KAI


185

# Muhammad Ali

In large numbers,
we disdain guys and gals
who, in spurts,
talk on and on about themselves
as if high insuperable winds.
We spurn braggadocios
who predict how destructive
as a crocodile they can be.
We usually dislike those
who dub themselves pretty
and use terms
vaingloriously.
We grimace at those
who call themselves great
and don themselves kings or queens.

But Ali . . . it's d-i-f-f-e-r-e-n-t . . .
He runs his own lively show.

No matter if he's verbose
and sings his greatness —
we who love him think him suave and cool.
We feel a love for people
seeping through his soul.
No matter if he says he's pretty —
we chuckle and agree.
We see it as truth
dressed in no real malice.
No matter if he talks destruction —
we cheer his prognostication,
and we egg him on
with his playful jest.
We see him as inoffensive
as a basking shark,
and we know behind it all
is just a clean-cut guy.

And always when Ali's fought,
we've hugged the TV screen,
or we've tried to snuggle close
toward a ringside seat.
We want him to be
as swift as a choice greyhound,
as powerful as a grizzly bear,
as pugnacious as a hornet,
and as wild as a lynx.
We who love Ali
have socked his opponent
with rights and lefts.
We've driven him against the ropes,
and we've pommeled him
with steel-clenched hands.
We've yelled and ferreted him
from any hiding place,
and sometimes we've
downed him,
and we've counted him out.

Our Ali is soberly unique.
Let him stage his extravaganza!
Let him be vociferous and bold.
Let him be impish
and a pure braggadocio.
Let him tease us and cajole us
and put us on.
Let him be histrionic
and a downright show.
Let his ways be brash
and his acts a butcherbird.
Let him be as harassing
as a jaeger,
and let his strength perforate.
He's a prize example
of a lovable man;

*(Continued)*     187

and win or lose,
he's a world's great champ.
He's king of the ring,
and he's "the greatest."

— NAOMI F. FAUST

*November, 1978*
*Two months after*
*his fight with Leon Spinks*

# the champ vs. coopman

here comes the champ muhammad ali
looking like a sleek black missile shot into the arena
followed by his fez-headed flock.
watch him psyche his foe like a
torpedo stalking a rowboat
he'll rope-a-dope the great white hope
to the tune of a thousand bills.
round one — his feet are faster than his fists
round two — coopman doesn't know what to do
round three — in a flash ali's gonna win the stash
round four — ali's showin' coopman the door
round five — is coopman still alive?
no, he's flat on the mat
'cause ali does float and sting.
he really does his thing when it comes to the ring.

—BETH BROWN PRESTON

# The Polishers of Brass

I am thinking of the men who polish brass in Georgetown;
bent over, their hands push back and forth with enormous
    force on each square inch.
So many doors, knobs, rails!
Men in their twenties, men in their sixties;
when they have gone all around and arrive at the place
    where they started, it has already tarnished, and they must
    begin again.

— TOI DERRICOTTE

# VIII

## *"In This Sad Space"*

"I will rise above
the chaos    rise w/YOU
w/ME    WE will
rise"

*(Cheryl Lynn Pastor [Cēlin])*

# Like a Phoenix

You are a
wonder
to me
generations removed
your back bent
and orphaned
under Charlie's whip
eyes lowered beneath his
hollow stare
like a phoenix
you rose

You are an
inspiration
to me
cities burned
your hands cuffed
and broken
by America's system
manhood castrated by its
many plagues
like a phoenix
you rose

You are a
blessing
to me
physical, emotional
societal threats
hounding your existence
Charlie's agents
turning your head
from your sisters
    to theirs
        to their brothers
            to their dope
without a doubt
like a phoenix
you'll rise

—SYBIL R. COLLINS

# frontline

*for Z.A.M.*

listen for the heat
of the spear in the wind
Black/burning/fury
      fury
     burning
    Black

listen for the heat
     *umkhonto we sizwe* &#42;
the spear in the wind
     *umkhonto we sizwe*
listen for the heat
of the spear in the wind
that's where you'll find him

look for the roar
     in the eye
     of the panther
Black/seething/hunger
hunger
seething
Black
look for the roar
     in the eye
     of the panther
you'll find him there

*listentothebeat/listentothebeat/listentothebeat*
              *of his freedom drum*
*listentothebeat/listentothebeat/listentothebeat*
              *of his freedom hum*

---

&#42;Umkhonto we sizwe: "Burning Spear" and/or "Spear of the Nation," Sabotage Wing of the African National Congress, formed in 1961 as a reaction to the violence of the oppressive and repressive South African System

194

touch his rhythm
and be renewed,
touch his rhythm and be renewed

he comes
a heat seeking missile
aimed at the heart
of a vicious racist System
a sharp dark scalpel cutting
               at the belly of a
        fat-cat/gut suckin System
        a soldier on the frontline
               soldier on the frontline

listen for the heat
        look for the roar
listen for the heat
        look for the roar 'cause
        Black grandma's eat a
               violent black death
        from hands of
        shotgun totin rabid dogs
        bearin eviction orders
               and tin badges
'cause Black bruthas die vicious
        black highway deaths at hands of
        chicken-shit/lynch-mob mentality/punks
               *and the System applauds them*
               *the System applauds them*

listen for the heat
        *umkhonto we sizwe*
look for the roar
        *umkhonto we sizwe*
a frontline soldier
        for the Cause

'cause sistuhs are framed/jailed/and/maimed
sistuhs *raped*
and the perps
afforded escape

*(Continued)*      

'cause our children are killed
by the *white girl's\* kiss*
and the System's Coffers are lined
with their bones
our children are killed
by the *white girl's kiss*
and the Coffers
are lined
with their bones

*listenfortheheat/lookfortheroar*
*listenfortheheat/lookfortheroar*
*listentothebeat/listentothebeat/listentothebeat* ...

touch
his rhythm
and be
renewed
touch
his rhythm
and be renewed

listen for the heat
of the spear in the wind
Black/burning/fury
fury
burning
Black

listen for the heat
*umkhonto we sizwe*
the spear in the wind
*umkhonto we sizwe*
listen for the heat
of the spear
in the wind
that's where you'll find him

---

*white girl: cocaine

196

listen
for the
heat
of the spear
in the wind

you'll find him there
you'll find him there

— A. WANJIKU H. REYNOLDS

# Search for Black Men: Vietnam Post-Mortem

Where did all the black men go?
I somehow fail to find
the rest who marched with Dr. King
and stood in picket lines.

> Where did my brothers disappear?
> My quandary stirs a tear
> for I recall with guns and tanks
> their faces, black, austere.

Where did they go — the brothers,
the uncles, dads, the lovers?
I see their hole gape squarely
in the circle of white "others."

> Snatched from their frat lines, meal lines, books,
> they went to Asia-land,
> retreating from their folks and fears
> to march on foreign sands.

I look about America:
their absence, a "black hole."
I seek some word of their demise, but
the story's still untold.

> For revelation of their plight,
> now that a score is spent,
> consult the scholars' history books
> to get a partial hint.

Some made it to the very top.
Some wrote a book or two.
Some conquered odds and dreamed The Dream
and got what they were due.

> A glance beneath a ghetto post
> or in the county jail
> is where some others ended up
> when life's great plan grew stale.

Some brothers flash to wartime scenes
and pace the world confused
while others stalk, stake out and stare
and prove they're not diffused.

> An autumn stroll through Arlington
> will find some still in line —
> or look in country churchyards
> beneath a birch or pine.

Some names you'll find on slabs of stone
that scream beyond the grave.
Reach out and touch the names inscribed;
recall the strong, the brave.

> Their hole in our society
> is evident and plain.
> The unborn that they were to bear
> are left no soul nor name.

Our outward wailing now has ceased,
but everywhere we see
their vacancy within our sight,
their missed intensity.

> They were to be our great black hope,
> strong-minded, post-degreed:
> Another tragic waste of race
> regardless of the deed.

— BEVERLY FIELDS BURNETTE

# Don't Listen

Beautiful Black man
Don't listen to the lies
Don't
listen
to the lies
about who you are
or ought to be
or could be
if you would be
Don't listen

Everlasting attempts to consume your testicles
make you doubt your self, your
experience, sanity, and manhood
Don't listen to the lies

From Africa to Indian land they tried
to convince you that you
were not all right
not worthy
and they
were
Do not listen to their lies
for they are skilled and well versed
in unthinkable deception
Pronouncing the lie while bible-sworn
they testify for each other
that atrocities never occurred and
they are so proud of their Indian blood and
smallpox in blankets was just a joke and
unsuspecting syphilitic Black men were born
to suffer anyway
so
where's the harm? After all,

they did it for the red, white, and
blue is the color of the underdog
Red is the blood that he lost, volunteered
in hope of acceptance
only to be told it was

not enough because
he
still lived and therefore must be
holding
back

White is the color of the cold
of the chill that wraps around
the Black man and
squeezes him till, frozen, it cracks
and falls
or the Black man crumbles
or comes out shooting .
only to be told
he did that wrong too cause
what will the widow do
with the children
and the bad memory
of the bad Black man
who thought he might find peace
on the other side
or that the sizzling of his skin for the feast
to which he was not invited
was more
than he was willing to permit

This
is
nightmare alley
nor is there hope somewhere
around the corner
or on Venus
that the white chill of the flag might warm
might feel something other than
fear at the sight of the blood
it has drawn, demanded
deceived others into spilling
Do **not** hope that one day
the white of the flag might discover
a soul, cause that's not
your soul and is clearly
their problem
Don't listen to them

*(Continued)*

Don't listen my brother
when they say
that you are not ok
When they run from your anger
it is their fear not yours
When they hide from your actions
it is their numbness not yours
When they vomit at the thought
of the passion that fuels you
it's their impotence not yours
Let them find passion . . . . next time
by choosing feelings
over greed and brutality

Do not listen
to the empty ones
who would trade you plastic
for the ivory of your teeth
or marbles for the gemstones
of your eyes
Who would sell you
charcoal as onyx
with statesmen verifying authenticity
Who push morsels into the cage
and expect gratitude.  No, adoration

Do not listen
when they act as if
you need them
Insisting that wet is dry
and no is yes
they destroy those
who expect limits to the lies
or an end in sight
or something suggesting
that nightmare alley is just an alley
and freedom is real and coming next week
to their neighborhood
Do not listen
to them


202

Regal redwood, ebony, mahogany
walnut and oak, all mirror your magnificence
Listen to the thunder shouting your power
Listen to the river roaring your glory
Listen to the tornado pounding your rhythm
You are
a god among gods
None can compare to the grace, the cosmic power
the passion and the manly sweetness
of you
Listen, my brother
to those who love you

— ABIMBOLA ADAMA

# Receptive Perspective
*For Bob: My Best Hope*

We have not always been in this sad space
From Khemit to Kentucky, Timbuctu to Tennessee,
from royalty and riches to soul-like poverty,
we have not always been in his sad space.

When you're made to disremember the prince you are within
and your woman is dismembered and they offer you her skin . . .
When your children are regarded as chips for poker games
and your mother is left salted down for vultures in hard rain . . . .
When you're brought to shores of stolen lands
and shown you cannot be a man . . . .
When the greed machine consumes your will
for yet another dollar bill . . . .
When all the laws of this fierce land
are crafted to chop off your hand,
leaving you numb, dexterity gone
and your wife moves on to a different song,
yet somehow, you still can run this race . . . . . .

Remember, brother,
we have not always been in this sad space.

— J.E.M. JONES

# The Mask

Hanging on the wall, an iron face watches me.
Snakes crawl up his cheeks
his eyes sink back to a land
where tales of warriors and empires
were woven into ancient tapestries, knotted to my blood.
He speaks to me beneath the tunes of Billie and Bessie.
I hear him *hum*\* the intervals in Coltrane,
reverberating the tales of men sold;
of women sold leaving earthen huts;
of children seized from villages
and brought to ships *waiting* on the water Niger.
Blue water witnessing:
*More blues* than the brownblack veins on Billie's arms.
*More blues* than the broken body of Bessie waiting
on a dusty southern backroad.
*More blues* than the last visions of Trane.
*More blues* than me walking through neon cities
walking through red southern fields,
not knowing where I belong.
The mask contains a deeper blues than those I know,
carving out my heart with yesterday's pain.

— IRMA MCCLAURIN

---

\*The italicized words are to be sung.

# Bring Them Home

350 thousand gone
to those bleak walls
where the bars clang shut
and sever body from soul.

This is American space-age savagery.
This — wake up! — this is the way,
this is the way, don't you see,
this is the way they split our family in two —
two drying, dying halves

Tortured in those steel dungeons,
our men throw their ripped-out hearts at us,
trophies of their pain,
torn flesh, life giving muscle,
hurled from cage to ghetto concentration camp
and back
and forth
and back
and forth.
The spaces between us become hazardously slick
with our own blood.
Oozing concession to powerlessness.
Seething testament of collaboration with the enemy.

The others watch this deathly ritual,
a confirmation of their success.

We must stop this.
We must stop this.
See through those lies called "criminal,"
called "pathological," called "recidivistic."
Call our men by their true names:
Father, Brother, Son, prisoners of war —
and bring them home.

— ANEB KGOSITSILE (GLORIA HOUSE)

# Of Men and Clouds

men like clouds must cry sometime
don't you think mama

if not for the murder of his brother
the beating of his mother
the rape of his woman/then when mama

if not for the countless revolutions/wars
he stood the loss of life for solutions of no color/
then when mama/am i not my brothers keeper/
when shall he cry/in time of hunger hollowing
not only his face but his mind/then when mama

oh how bitterly we watch as he drags his defensive nature
to kneel castrated before colorless gods
with tongues of contempt/must i watch mama
how mama can i turn my cheek when men like clouds
must cry sometime

men like clouds must cry sometime/don't you wonder mama
his mother dries tender swellings before they form
and the fatherless child is told men don't dare
his woman defiles his name bringing slander
to his stonehead grave nailed shut at tender ages
oh spare his back

how mama must my brother express his feelings
when whipped draped in chains/beaten jobless/bruised penniless
purposely wounded by a bleeding heart of no tears/
only the pain remains — gift not with scars for his knowing/
how mama/we watch him stand with broken will
before odorless steel bars that absorb only the coldness
of his sweat/nothing of the swelling of his eye

must i watch mama

how

when then will we allow men
like clouds
to cry sometime

— SHIRLEY HAYDEN-WHITLEY

208

# To the Black Man
### (From one who loves him, a Black woman)

**I.**
I am not
your
enemy

Don't you remember . . . ?

I was sold
w/YOU
into slavery     into bondage
I suffered
w/YOU
the loss of family     of identity
I forged
w/YOU
a new identity
of pride and dignity
I bled
w/YOU
from the lash     the whip
I toiled
w/YOU
in the fields     in the houses . . .
with YOUR baby strapped
to MY back
I sang
w/YOU
of freedom from bondage
I led armies
of/YOU
to freedom on my railroad . . . underground . . .

**II.**
I went to battle
for/YOU
to put an end
to YOUR lynching

*(Continued)*     

for the
abolishment of "Jim Crow"
I cried
w/YOU
when OUR children
were stolen from MY
body
for/YOU
when YOU
were stolen from MY
arms
to/YOU
when I
was stolen from YOUR
body
YOUR
arms
YOUR
love . . . and raped . . .

Don't you remember . . . ?

**III.**
I have always fought
w/YOU
stood
by/YOU
marched
w/YOU
My body was
blown apart
by bombs
I went to
jail
was shot at
beaten . . .
My eyes were
gassed
I
rioted . . . all
w/YOU

**IV.**
I screamed
lamented
in pain when
YOU
tore away from MY
body
into a world
I would spend MY
life
defending you to . . .
I worked
my whole life
to raise
YOU
prayed
for/YOU
sang
to/YOU
healed YOUR
wounds
gave YOU
my
body in support of
OUR cause
raised my fist
w/YOU

Don't you remember . . . ?

I am not
your
enemy


**V.**
When YOU choose to
leave ME to raise
OUR children
it is YOUR
future YOU
are hurting

*(Continued)*     211

I am not the
source
of YOUR
hurt        your
anguish        your
pain and humiliation
I too
am a
victim

Don't you remember . . . ?

I am not
your
enemy . . .

I am not
afraid
of YOU
I have earned
YOUR respect
YOU will earn
mine    YOU
will not frighten
ME
away

I will love
YOU        care
for/YOU
fight by YOUR side
w/YOU
heal
YOUR wounds        share
YOUR pain
I will rise above
the chaos
the systematic
destruction
of US
I will survive
w/YOU        cry

w/YOU      stand
against a common enemy
w/YOU . . .
I will rise above
the chaos
I will rise above
w/YOU
if you will only
let ME
I will rise above
the chaos     rise w/YOU
w/ME     **WE** will
rise

I am not
your
enemy

Don't you remember . . . ?

— CHERYL LYNN PASTOR (CĒLIN)

# Warriors  Welcome

Black man
    come home
i miss you
    i need you
just as much as you need me
with you not against you
Black man
    i love you
come home
we've been apart too long
too long a part of a culture
other than our own
too long chained
to foreign ideologies
socializing schemes
too long beaten
dragged a prisoner thru a concept
a time when i too was angry
    fighting
calling on violence
being all the things
African women are
when African man is in jeopardy

remnants of
    broken families
    broken spirits
    broken dreams
    broken backs
from sun up to sun down
    broken necks
from inside jail cells
damned us to a living hell
but i clearly understood
surfacing all my inner strength
as only an African woman could

i eternalized the womb
the mother of Frederick Douglass
i conceptualized the spirit

214

of Amy Garvey
i became the love Shaka cuddled
as Sojourner
i  too stepped into
the light of the truth

thru Harriet Tubman's
underground railroad
i rode . . .
        down the Nile
        the Niger
i comprehended
        Queen Candace
            Ann Nzinga
                Queen Hatshepsut
                    Nefertiti
i brought back with me
the blues & soul of Bessie and Billie
no more strange fruit
bitter leaves
black bodies hanging from
the limbs of trees
goodbye heart ache
we can put the blues on the run

just
come home
come home
all you makers of Malcolm
        men of Hannibal
        sons of King
i know
i know you have
Nat Turner dreams

Black man
say you're tired
say you're tired of
        white powder
        white thighs
three-piece suits
stiff collars and ties

Black man
say you're tired
say you're coming home
to stay


— PHAVIA KUJICHAGULIA

# Acknowledgments

*Grateful acknowledgment is made to the publications listed below and to the authors who granted their permission to reprint the following poems:*

Abimbola Adama: "Don't Listen" from *Gifts from the Spirit* by Abimbola Adama: (Black Angels Press, 1991).

Monifa Atungaye: "For My Brother" and "The Blacksmith" from *Provisions* by Monifa Atungaye (Lotus Press, 1989).

Avotcja: "Papi Was a Dancing Man" from *Reggae Calendar International* (August, 1990); "Max Roach/The Rhythm Wizard" from *Pura Candela/Pure Fire* by Avotcja (LaRaza Graphics, 1991).

Melba Joyce Boyd: "sunflowers and saturdays" from *Cat Eyes and Dead Wood* by Melba Joyce Boyd (Fallen Angel Press, 1978); "To Darnell and Johnny" from *The Broadside Series (*No. 68, 1973), reprinted in *Cat Eyes and Dead Wood;* "The League of Defense" from *City Arts Quarterly* (Vol. IV, No. 1/2)), reprinted in *The Inventory of Black Roses* by Melba Joyce Boyd (Past Tents Press, 1989).

Jill Witherspoon Boyer: "George Jackson" from *Breaking Camp* by Jill Witherspoon Boyer (Lotus Press, 1984).

Karla Francesca Brundage: "Peaches" from *Konch* (August, 1991).

Pearl Cleage: "Blue Lights in the Basement" (Part I of "Motown Suite") and "Summer Is Coming" from *The Brass Bed and Other Stories* by Pearl Cleage (Third World Press, 1991).

Linda Cousins: "marley no die" from *This Ancestral Poetsong: Poetworks of Black History, Love, Laughter, and Life* (audiotape) by Linda Cousins (The Universal Black Writer Press, 1989).

(Malika) Odessa Davis: "The Clothes You Color" from *Growth of a Serious Black Woman* (The Society of African American Poets Association of Detroit, 1989).

Toi Derricotte: "In Knowledge of Young Boys" from *Natural Birth* by Toi Derricotte (Crossing Press, 1983); "Before Making Love" and "The Polishers of Brass" from *Captivity* by Toi Derricotte (University of Pittsburgh Press, 1989).

Naomi F. Faust: "As I Recount My Love" from *And I Travel by Rhythms and Words* by Naomi F. Faust (Lotus Press, 1990); "Martin Luther King" from *Speaking in Verse* by Naomi F. Faust (Branden Press, 1974), reprinted in *And I Travel by Rhythms and Words*; "Muhammad Ali" from *The New York Amsterdam News* (September 27, 1980), reprinted in *All Beautiful Things* by

217

Naomi F. Faust (Lotus Press, 1983) and in *And I Travel by Rhythms and Words.*

Nikki Giovanni: "Beautiful Black Men" from *Black Judgment* by Nikki Giovanni (Broadside Press, 1968). By permission of the author.

Maketa Groves: "Katumwbe" from *Morena* (1983).

Karen Halliburton: "Just Love" and "On the Edges" from *You Know* by Karen Halliburton (Warrior Chant Press, 1991).

Shirley Hayden-Whitley: "Of Men and Clouds" (originally "Of Men and Tears") from *Interlock* (1990/91).

Beverly Jarrett: "Sam" from *Some of My Best Friends Are Men* by Beverly Jarrett (Black Angels Press, 1992).

Regina B. Jennings: "To Langston" from *Steppingstones* (Winter, 1984).

Nubia Kai: "Nat Turner," "Joe Louis," "Malcolm," and "Papa" from *Solos* by Nubia Kai (Lotus Press, 1988).

Sybil Kein: "Robert Hayden," "Louie," and "B.B. King" from *Visions from the Rainbow* by Sybil Kein (N.D. Hosking, 1979), reprinted in *Delta Dancer* by Sybil Kein (Lotus Press, 1984). "Leadbelly," "Barbecue Bob Hicks,"and "Jelly Roll Morton" from *Delta Dancer.*

Dolores Kendrick: "For My Father on the Gift of Another Eye" and "Uncle Gus" from *Now Is the Thing to Praise* by Dolores Kendrick (Lotus Press, 1984).

Aneb Kgositsile (Gloria House): "Bring Them Home," "Direction," and "I Am Willie or Amos" from *Blood River* by Aneb Kgositsile (Gloria House) (Broadside Press, 1983); "For Uri at 16," "Mandala for Mandela," For Kyasa, Little Brother," and "Love Dreadlocked" from *Rainrituals* by Aneb Kgositsile (Gloria House) (Broadside Press, 1990).

Phavia Kujichagulia: "Warriors Welcome," "Romance," and "Black Satin Stallion" (from *Undercover or Overexposed* by Phavia Kujichagulia (A. Wisdom Company, 1989).

Pinkie Gordon Lane: "Four Poems for Gordon" from *I Never Scream: New and Selected Poems* by Pinkie Gordon Lane (Lotus Press, 1985).

Naomi Long Madgett: "Black Poet," "'The Sun Do Move,'" and "October Lament" from *Octavia and Other Poems* by Naomi Long Madgett (Third World Press, 1988).

Irma McClaurin: "The Mask" from *Obsidian* (1976); "You Are Like the Coming of Dawn" from *Song in the Night* by Irma McClaurin (Pearl Press, 1974); both reprinted in *Pearl's Song* by Irma McClaurin (Lotus Press, 1988).

May Miller: "My Father" from *The Clearing and Beyond* (Charioteer Press, 1974); "For Robert Hayden," "Alain LeRoy Locke," and "The

218

Janitor (Circa 1940)" from "Saturday Night" from *The Ransomed Wait* by May Miller (Lotus Press, 1983); all reprinted in *Collected Poems* by May Miller (Lotus Press, 1989).

Gloria Oden: "Resurrections (#36)" from *Resurrections* by Gloria Oden (Oliphant Press, 1978).

Beth Brown Preston: "all the brothers," "little mecca" and "the champ vs. coopman" from *Lightyears: Poems 1973-1976* by Beth Brown (Lotus Press, 1982); "On Witnessing the Receipt of an Honorary Degree by Sterling Brown" from *Satin Tunnels* by Beth Brown (Lotus Press, 1989).

Johari Mahasin Rashad: "Sisterlove 1" from *Hoo-Doo* (No. 5), reprinted in *(R)Evolutions* by Johari Mahasin Rashad (Writely So!, 1982); "Search" from *(R)Evolutions;* "My Gift to You" from *Woman, too* by Johari Mahasin Rashad (Writely So!, 1984).

A. Wanjiku H. Reynolds: "j. harrington" and "herman" from *Cognac and Collard Greens* by A. Wanjiku H. Reynolds (1985); "frontline" and "cousin george" from *A Gathering of Hands* by A. Wanjiku H. Reynolds (1990), both published by Ngoma's Gourd, Inc.

Lucy E. Thornton-Berry: "Harry's Afro Hut," "Who's Really Got the Power?" and "Never on Prime Time" from *From Survivin to Thrivin* by Lucy E. Thornton-Berry (C.H. Fairfax Company, 1990).

Paulette Childress White: "This Warrior" and "Oronde" from *Love Poem to a Black Junkie* by Paulette Childress White (Lotus Press, 1975).

# Biographical Notes

**Abimbola Adama**, a resident of Palo Alto, CA, is a poet, writer, and educator who delights in helping others to find "their own inner magnificence." She teaches meditation and believes that "being African American is a gift from loving gods who appreciate passion, style, and genius wrapped in the vibrating beauty of color."

**Opal Palmer Adisa** is a poet, playwright, and storyteller. Currently residing in Oakland, CA, her roots are in Jamaica. She considers herself a "Ja-American." Her published works are *Pina, the Many-Eyed Fruit* (Julian Richardson Associates, 1985), *Bake-Face and Other Guava Stories* (Kelsey Street Press, 1986), and *Traveling Woman*, poems with Devorah Major (Jukebox Press, 1989).

**Kenyette Adrine-Robinson** is poet-in-residence with the Department of Pan-African Studies at Kent State University and lives in Cleveland, OH. Working with the Pan-African community worldwide, writing, and teaching keep her busy. Her two books of poetry are *Thru Kenyette Eyes* and *Be My Shoo-gar*.

**Collette Armstead** has been a fiction fellow of the Ragdale Foundation and a 1986 and 1987 recipient of the Northeastern Illinois University Publication Scholarship. She was also awarded a Neighborhood Arts Program grant in 1988 and a Community Arts Assistance Program grant in 1991. She has recently moved to Norfolk, VA where she continues her work on a collection of poetry to be entitled, *Dream Scenes: A Gathering of Poems*.

**Monifa Atungaye** is the recipient of a McKnight Doctoral Fellowship and is currently pursuing her Ph.D. degree in English with an emphasis on writing and critical theory at Florida State University in Tallahassee. She is also director of Free Zone Productions; a video of her company's work, "Reunion," was recently produced for public television to be aired later this year. She is author of *Provisions*, a volume of poetry (Lotus Press, 1989).

**Burniece Avery** is author of *Walk Quietly Through the Night and Cry Softly* (Balamp, 1977), an historical non-fiction book which is on the recommended reading list of many school systems. Presently a resident of Las Vegas, NV, she continues with her writing with recent contributions appearing in *Senior Voice*.

221

**Avotcja** (pronounced *uh-VAH-cha*) represents the fourth generation of performing artists in her family. She is a poet, storyteller, musician, photographer, and craftswoman. She is also an educator, teaching creative writing, music, and Pan-African history in public schools and prisons. A disk jockey on KPOO-FM in San Francisco, CA, and KPFA-FM in Berkeley, she also writes a monthly column for *Reggae Calendar International.* She is vice-president of International Black Writers and Artists, Local #5 and staff storyteller for Word Conjurors.

**Melba Joyce Boyd,** who once served as an editor at Broadside Press, is associate professor of Afro-American Studies at the University of Michigan at Flint. Dr. Boyd is author of four books of poetry: *Cat Eyes and Dead Wood, Song for Maya, Thirteen Frozen Flamingoes,* and *The Inventory of Black Roses. Song for Maya* was translated for a German edition in 1989 (WURF Verlag Press). Her work has appeared in various journals and periodicals and has been anthologized.

**Jill Witherspoon Boyer** is the author of two collections of poetry, *Dream Farmer* (Broadside Press, 1975) and *Breaking Camp* (Lotus Press, 1984). Much of her creative energy now is directed toward photography. A native of Detroit holding a master's degree in social work, she now makes her home in Inglewood, CA with her husband and teenage daughter, Malaika.

**Karla Francesca Brundage** was born in Berkeley, CA but spent most of her early years in Hawaii, which she still considers her home. Educated at Vassar College, she focused on African literature in the English language. She is currently a resident of Oakland, CA.

**Beverly Fields Burnette**, a 1968 graduate of Livingstone College, resides in Raleigh, NC with her daughters Tara and Teri. An elementary school guidance counselor, she has done freelance writing and script-writing for local children's television. She has also edited a children's advice column and acted in local children's theater.

**Marilyn Elain Carmen (Aisha Eshe)**, who currently lives in Philadelphia, PA, was a 1990 recipient of a fellowship in literature from the Pennsylvania State Council on the Arts. She is author of a novella, *Blood at the Root* (Esoterica Press, 1990), and her poems have been widely published.

**Pearl Cleage** is an Atlanta-based writer who currently serves as editor of *Catalyst* Magazine. She is also artistic director of Just Us Theater

Company. She is author of two books, *Mad at Miles: A Blackwoman's Guide to Truth* and *The Brass Bed and Other Stories* (Third World Press, 1991). She has one daughter, Deignan.

**Sibyl Rae Collins** won a Detroit Public Schools writing award for her first short story when she was eight years old. She continues to write in all genres. In addition, she enjoys acting. She is a native of Detroit, where she still makes her home.

**Jayne Cortez** is the author of eight books of poetry, including *Poetic Magnetic*, and producer of five recordings of poetry, the most recent of which is *Everywhere Drums*. She is recipient of the American Book Award, the New York Artists Foundation Award for poetry, and The National Endowment for the Arts award. Her poems have been widely published in journals, magazines, and anthologies and translated into many languages. She has lectured and read her poetry throughout the United States, Africa, Europe, Latin America, and the Caribbean. Born in Arizona and reared in California, she is now a resident of New York City. (See *Dictionary of Literary Biography: Afro-American Poets Since 1955*, Vol. 41, pp. 69-74).

**Linda Cousins** is an award-winning poet, historical researcher, and teacher. Her literary works have appeared on stage, radio, television, and in video productions, the most recent being *The Mystical Experiences of Harriet Tubman* and *The Caribbean: A Cultural Journey.* She is also publisher and editor of The Universal Black Writer Press of Brooklyn, NY, where she lives.

**Stella Crews** is co-editor of *HIPology,* an anthology of poetry by Detroiters (Broadside Press, 1990) and author of two books of her own poems, *Thieves, or The Laundromat Bandit* (Thorne Publications, 1982) and *Salad in August* (Ridgeway Press, 1990). A resident of Detroit, she has been writing since 1969. She is currently editing an anthology of prose by women of color to be entitled, *Womyn in Exile,* to be published by Wayne State University Press. Ms. Crews is the mother of a fifteen-year-old daughter.

**(Malika) Odessa Davis** is founder and president of SOAPAD (Society of African American Poets Association of Detroit). Her writings cover the entire spectrum of human life: politics, love, drugs, religion, mental health, and education. She has performed her poems for churches, schools, and youth homes, and in night clubs of various cities. She resides in Detroit.

**Toi Derricotte** is the author of three books of poetry: *The Empress of the Death House* (Lotus Press, 1978), *Natural Birth* (Crossing Press, 1983), and *Captivity* (University of Pittsburgh Press, 1989). She is recipient of two fellowships from The National Foundation of the Arts, a Pushcart Prize, and the Lucille Medwick Award from the Poetry Society of America. A native of Detroit, she presently resides in Potomac, MD.

**Naomi F. Faust** is the author of three books of poetry: *Speaking in Verse* (Branden Press, 1974): *All Beautiful Things* (Lotus Press, 1983); and *And I Travel by Rhythms and Words* (Lotus Press, 1990). Her poems have won various awards, including one from the International Poets Academy which named her International Eminent Poet. Dr. Faust has served as professor at Queens College of the City University of New York. She resides in Jamaica, NY.

**Nikki Giovanni** is the author of numerous books of poetry and prose, including *My House* (Morrow, 1972), *Cotton Candy on a Rainy Day* (Morrow, 1978), and *Those Who Ride the Night Winds* (Morrow, 1983), and has enjoyed a popularity as writer and lecturer which few poets have experienced. Emerging as one of the strong voices of the Sixties, her work has mellowed and maintained its appeal, especially for the young to whom much of her poetry is directed. She believes that "only the healing education of literature will gentle the struggles of humankind." She is currently teaching at the Virginia Polytechnic Institute and State University in Blacksburg, VA. (See the *Dictionary of Literary Biography: Afro-American Poets Since 1955*, Vol. 41, pp. 135-151.)

**Maketa Groves** is a native of Detroit who now resides in San Francisco where she is working on a novel. Her father, she writes, who taught her her first poem when she was seven, remains "the most positive force in my life."

**Karen Halliburton** is the author of one book of poetry, *You Know* (Warrior Chant Press, 1991). She describes her work as "raw w/a message." She holds a degree in business management from William Paterson College in New Jersey and an A.A.S. from the Fashion Institute of Technology in New York. She is director of information for *Essence* magazine and lives in Hackensack, NJ.

**Shirley Hayden-Whitley** is a poet, essayist, and organizer who lives in Lexington, KY. Her books of poetry are *It's My Poetry and I'll Cry If I Want To* (1989); *Home* (1990); and *Natural Floods* (1991). Her short story collections include *Sometimes Life Ain't Sweet, You Know* (1991) and *Lesbian Tales of Stephen Foster* to be published in the fall of 1992.

**Elana Hayes,** a native of Detroit, is currently pursuing her B.A. degree in English at University of Detroit Mercy. She aspires to a career in broadcast media writing and poetry. She is married and the mother of a toddler son.

**Beverly Jarrett** is a poet and playwright residing in Oakland, CA. Her first book of poetry is *Some of My Best Friends Are Men* (Black Angels Press, 1992). She has been featured in many readings and received an award from the Oakland Ensemble Theatre to spend a month at Dorland Arts Colony near San Diego. She is a native of St. Louis, MO where her daughter Kimberly now attends college.

**Regina B. Jennings** is a professor of English at Franklin and Marshall College, and she is completing her doctoral dissertation at Temple University. Her work has appeared in such publications as *Essence, Shooting Star Review, Catalyst,* and *Language and Literature in the African-American Imagination.* Four manuscripts are awaiting publication. Ms. Jennings lives in Philadelphia.

**J.E.M. Jones,** a native New Yorker, has had poems published in four countries and at least twenty states. Her sons' names, Rael and Avery, she writes, are a statement. By their meanings, she hopes that they may strive to be committed "to self-growth, universal respect, and productive love." She lives in Hollis, NY and is a widow.

**Nubia Kai** is a multi-talented writer who feels equally comfortable with poetry, fiction, and drama. As an undergraduate and graduate student at Wayne State University, she won three Tompkins awards, two in drama and one in fiction. She has received three Creative Artist awards from the Michigan Council for the Arts and a poetry award from the National Endowment of the Arts. She is author of two books of poetry, *Peace of Mind* (Pajoma Press) and *Solos* (Lotus Press, 1988), and her work has appeared in anthologies and numerous journals. She has recently moved to Senegal.

**Sybil Kein,** a New Orleans Creole poet, playwright, and musician, is a pioneer in the use of the Louisiana Creole language in literature and

225

promotes the Creole culture through original works and scholarship. Her five books of poetry include *Gombo People* (1981) and *Delta Dancer* (Lotus Press, 1984). Dr. Kein is professor of English at The University of Michigan at Flint.

**Dolores Kendrick** has travelled broadly, teaching in Hawaii and Spain and serving as poet-in-residence at several schools and colleges in this country and in Shanghai, China. She was also a Fullbright scholar in Northern Ireland. Currently the Vira I. Heinz Professor at Phillips Exeter Academy, she maintains her residence in Washington, D.C. She has won two YADDO fellowships and a National Endowment of the Arts Award. Her books of poetry include *Through the Ceiling* (Paul Breman, London, 1975), *Now Is the Thing to Praise* (Lotus Press, 1984), and *The Women of Plums* (William Morrow, 1989), the last of which won the Wolf-Anisfield Award in 1990 and was named the New York Public Library Best Book for Teenagers.

**Aneb Kgositsile (Gloria House)** was educated at the University of California-Berkeley and The University of Michigan, where she earned the Ph.D. degree. She is associate professor of humanities at Wayne State University and is active in political and cultural organizations. A resident of Detroit, she is author of two books of poetry, *Blood River* (1983) and *Rainrituals* (1990), both published by Broadside Press.

**Phavia Kujichagulia** is a writer, performance artist, musician, dancer, educator, and mother of twins. As founder and executive director of A. Wisdom Company in Oakland, CA, she has published four books of poetry, including *Undercover or Overexposed* (1989), and produced two albums of her work. She is also author of *Kindred Spirits*, a novel.

**Pinkie Gordon Lane** was the first black woman to earn a Ph.D. degree at Louisiana State University and is presently the Poet Laureate of that state, the first African-American to be so honored. In 1991 she was inducted into the Louisiana Black History Hall of Fame. She is the former English department head at Southern Illinois University in Baton Rouge, LA and is now professor emerita of that institution. Her poems have appeared in numerous literary journals, and she has read throughout the nation and four countries of Africa. Dr. Lane's collections of poems include *Wind Thoughts* (1972), *The Mystic Female* (1978), and *I Never Scream : New and Selected Poems* (Lotus Press, 1985), and *Girl at the Window* (1991). (See *Dictionary of Literary Biography: Afro-American Poets Since 1955*, Vol. 41.)

226

**Naomi Long Madgett** published the first of her seven books of poetry in 1941 at the age of seventeen. Her more recent collections include *Pink Ladies in the Afternoo*n (1972), *Exits and Entrances* (1978), both by Lotus Press, and *Octavia and Other Poems* (Third World Press, 1988). The last title became the first book of poetry to ever become "required" reading in the public high schools of Detroit. Dr. Madgett's poems have appeared in numerous journals and more than one hundred anthologies in this country and abroad. Some have been translated into five European languages and several set to music and publicly performed. She is professor emerita of English at Eastern Michigan University and director and editor of Lotus Press, Inc. in Detroit, where she resides. (See *Dictionary of Literary Biography: Afro-American Writers 1940-1955*, Vol. 76, pp. 104-112.

**Maria Madison,** a native of Angeles City in the Phillipines, is married and lives in New London, CT. "Even Though We Never Went Camping" is the first of her poems to be published.

**Devorah Major**, a Californian by birth, writes poetry, fiction, and essays. She is co-author (with Opal Palmer Adisa) of one book of poems, *Travelling Woman*. She has won a California Arts Council writing fellowship and Pushcart Prize recognition and is currently working on her first novel. Ms. Major lives in San Francisco.

**Irma McClaurin** received her B.A. degree in American studies from Grinnell College in 1973 and her M.F.A. at the University of Massachusetts at Amherst in 1976. She is currently pursuing her Ph.D. in anthropology. Her poems have appeared in magazines and anthologies, and several have been translated into Swedish and Spanish. Her two books of poetry are *Song in the Night* (Pearl Press, 1974) and *Pearl's Song* (Lotus Press, 1988). Ms. McClaurin resides in Amherst, MA.

**May Miller,** the third of five children of the legendary Dean Kelly Miller, grew up on the campus of Howard University. A minor literary figure of the Harlem Renaissance, she was also involved in the Negro Little Theater Movement, one of her plays winning an *Opportunity* magazine award in 1925. In 1944 she returned to Washington after teaching in Baltimore for twenty years and married the late John Lewis Sullivan. The following year she made her debut as a poet. Her numerous readings include the Library of Congress, the Smithsonian Institution, and the Folger Shakespeare Library. Ms. Miller has served on various literature advisory panels and boards. Her work has been widely published, and she has received numerous honors. Her nine books of poetry include *Into the Clearing* (The Charioteer Press, 1959); *Halfway to the Sun*, children's poems (Washington Writers' Publishing House, 1981); *Dust of Uncertain Journey* (1975), *The Ransomed Wait* (1983) and *Collected Poems* (1989), the last three published by Lotus Press. Ms. Miller lives in Washington, D.C. (See *Dictionary of Literary Biography: Afro-American Poets Since 1955*, Vol. 41, pp. 241-247).

**Gloria Oden** is a professor of English at The University of Maryland, Baltimore County. She also specializes in research into pre-Civil War black American history. Dr. Oden has held fellowships from the John Hay Whitney Foundation and YADDO. Her most recent book of poetry is *The Tie That Binds* (Oliphant Press, 1980).

**Cheryl Lynn Pastor (Cēlin),** born in Jacksonville, FL, has been a resident of Detroit since 1961. Her work has been published in *Michigan Citizen* and *PAMBANA, Journal of World Affairs*. She lives with her parents and is employed by the City of Detroit.

**Erica Annette Pierce** is a 1978 graduate of Central State University where she received a number of writing awards. In 1989 she received the Paul Laurence Dunbar Award from the Detroit Black Writers Guild. A former reporter for the *Detroit Legal News,* she is now working on her first novel. She resides in Detroit.

**Beth Brown Preston,** a resident of Philadelphia, is the author of numerous articles and reviews, and her poetry has been widely published. She has participated in the Pennsylvania Poets-in-the-Schools Program and received several awards, including the *Callaloo* Creative Writing Award in poetry and a CBS fellowship in writing. Among her collections of poetry are *Lightyears: Poems 1973-1976* (Lotus Press, 1982), *Kaze* (Overtone Series, 1985), *Bouquets* (Overtone Series, 1986), and *Satin Tunnels* (Lotus Press, 1989).

**Johari Mahasin Rashad**, a native and resident of Washington, D.C., is a member of the African-American Writers' Guild, the National Writers' Union, the International Women's Writing Guild, and Washington Independent Writers. Her published works are *(R)Evolutions* (1982), *Woman, too* (1984), both published by Writely So!, and *Steppin'Over the Glass: Life Journeys in Poetry and Prose* (1992).

**Leslie Reese** is author of one book of poetry, *Upside Down Tapestry Mosaic History* (Broadside Press, 1987), and the 1991 recipient of the Rising Star Award from the Renaissance Chapter of The Links, Inc. Her work has appeared in *Solid Ground, a New World Journal; City Arts Quarterly; Detroit Metro Times; Obsidian II*; and *Michigan Quarterly Review.* A former Detroiter, Ms. Reese now resides in Huntsville, AL.

**A. Wanjiku H. Reynolds,** a resident of the South Bronx and a mother, is a member of Women of the First World Collective and FrontLine. She is also the founder of Ngoma's Gourd, Inc. Her works have appeared in a number of publications, including *New Rain, Literati Internazionale, NOBO Magazine, Catalyst,* and *Essence.* She is author of two books of poetry, *Cognac and Collard Greens (1985)* and *A Gathering of Hands (tryin to keep time & trying to make a difference)* (1990).

**Satiafa (Vivian Verdell Gordon)** is a professor in the Department of Africana Studies at the State University of New York at Albany. She is the author of four books, including one collection of poetry, *For Dark Women and Others* (Lotus Press, 1983).

**Rosalie Shannon,** originally from Des Moines, IA, has been a resident of Detroit since 1952. She is the mother of three sons and a daughter. Three of her children are in college and one in military service. After almost twenty years, she returned to school and received her B.A. degree at University of Detroit in 1988. She is presently employed as a job developer and training specialist for the City of Detroit. "Seasons" is her first publication.

**Jennifer E. Smith** is coordinator of the University of the District of Columbia Poetry Series and editor and publisher of *Black Arts Bulletin.* She was the winner of the 1991 Mount Vernon College Poetry Festival. Her poems have appeared in various journals, including *Catalyst, Black American Literature Forum*, and *Obsidian II.* She is a resident of Washington, D.C.

**Lucy E. Thornton-Berry,** a native and resident of Baltimore, is a graduate of Livingstone College in Salisbury, NC. A librarian, she is the creator of the Liquorice Stick Kids, positive image dolls. Mrs. Thornton-Berry is also the author of one book of poetry, *From Survivin to Thrivin* (C.H. Fairfax Company, 1990).

**Hilda Vest** is the present publisher of Broadside Press. She has been a winner of the poetry contest sponsored by Detroit Women Writers and a scholarship to the Cranbrook Writers' Conference. A graduate of Wayne State University, Mrs. Vest is a retired teacher in Detroit Public Schools for which she has served as facilitator at the Young Authors Conference. She was also a presenter at the Martin Luther King Day Symposium held at The University of Michigan. She is listed in *Who's Who Among Black Americans*.

**Roxanne Whitaker** is a young poet who wants her writing "to transcend paper and speak." She feels that, "as a people, we need more light-workers, not pretenders to a rigid throne or slaves to unbending ideas and elitist cliques. Mentors. Accessibility. Truth." Ms. Whitaker resides in Brooklyn.

**Greta White** lives in Wilmington, DE with her two children, Tara and T.J., whom she calls "my motivation and inspiration." Presently employed as an administrative officer with Wachovia Corporation, she continues to engage in the writing which she has loved since childhood.

**Paulette Childress White** is author of two books of poetry, *Love Poem to a Black Junkie* (1984) and *The Watermelon Dress: Portrait of a Woman* (1984), both published by Lotus Press. Her short stories have been published in such magazines as *Redbook* and *Essence* and included in several anthologies. A resident of Detroit and mother of five sons, she received her education at Wayne State University where she is completing her requirements for the Ph.D. degree. She is presently teaching at Henry Ford Community College in Dearborn.

**Wanda Winbush** holds a B.A. degree in sociology and an M.A. in counseling. A native and resident of Washington, D.C., she is a member of the African-American Writers Guild. Her work has been published in periodicals such as *New Directions*, *Hilltonian*, and *Georgian* magazines, as well as in various anthologies. She received honorable mention in the ninth annual Larry Neal Writers' Competition for criticism.

# Index of Authors and Titles

232

234

# Excerpts from Book Reviews

"This exceptional anthology of poetry from 55 writers arrives at a most crucial time when the males of an entire race are in physical and spiritual jeopardy *by design* . . . . There are so many well-crafted pieces, startling in their clarity, that it is often difficult to affix them to their assigned sections . . . . [They] rumbled through this reviewer like a springtime thunderstorm, eliciting strong responses and memories . . . . The women offer hope and solace."

(Terri L. Jewell, *Capital Times*)

"Evocative and thought-provoking, the poems . . . effectively fill a void in black literature."

(Sarah Sue Goldsmith, Baton Rouge *Magazine)*

"This poetry overall is both accessible and accomplished. This is a valuable collection of voices that speak with strength, positive feeling, poetic passion . . . . a surprising outpouring of tribute considering the bleakness of the history in which African-American males have struggled to claim their identity."

(Naomi S. Myrvaagnes, *Kliatt Young Adult Paperback Book Guide*)

"With so many titles pinpointing problems, it's refreshing to consider a strong celebration which expresses compassion and support for the black male."

*(The Bookwatch)*

"The reception of *Adam of Ifé* demonstrates that African-Americans are pausing to examine sexual politics and their impact on the black community. There is a growing determination to look beyond the frustration and to heal the scars caused by painful relationships. All sisters and brothers can identify the scars, but there are increasing numbers of people who believe that we can become empowered to resolve our conflicts."

(Dr. Brenda Wall, clinical psychologist, as quoted by Toni Y. Joseph in *The Dallas Morning News,* "Ode to Black Men.")